Praise for *The Intelligent Leader*

"John Mattone understands that truly great leadership always starts on the inside. More than that, John is a master of helping people discover and cultivate their innate leadership potential through advice that is both practical and profound. His new book, *The Intelligent Leader*, beautifully illuminates the heart of great leadership through seven secrets that can have the biggest and brightest impact on the world."

—Deepak Chopra, author, *You Are the Universe*

"Great leadership is rare. The reason is simple—most people don't have a methodology for developing their leadership skills. In his new book, John Mattone skillfully and succinctly fills that void. It is a must-read for those in any walk of life who want to enhance their leadership skills and have fun doing so."

—Hap Klopp, founder, The North Face; author, *Almost: 12 Electric Months Chasing A Silicon Valley Dream*

"John has composed the go-to guide for leaders, new and experienced. He has distilled his wisdom into easy-to-follow modules for leaders to be both effective and inspiring. He covers everything from self-concept, influencing others, daily skills, development, culture, and courage. This book should sit on every leader's desk."

—Dr. Marcia Reynolds, author, *The Discomfort Zone: How Leaders Turn Difficult Conversations into Breakthroughs*

"In *The Intelligent Leader*, John Mattone shares wisdom from his years of executive coaching in a practical and thought-provoking guide for leaders at all levels. His leadership framework is both elegant in its simplicity and profound in its depth. If you have a genuine desire to dive deep, ask hard questions, and do what it takes to achieve your potential as a leader, the insights in this book will equip you well for the journey."

—Kathy Mazzarella, chairman, president, and CEO, Graybar

"It's rare that you come across wisdom so clear and compelling that it shocks you out of your day-to-day mindset and shows you the possibility of doing something truly remarkable with your life and career. John Mattone does just that with his new book, which stands out among the many leadership titles as a rare gem of deep and practical guidance on the path to becoming a better leader—and human being."

—Raúl Ibáñez, ESPN baseball analyst and former MLB All-Star

"This fast-moving, practical book shows you how to take complete charge of your life, achieve your goals, and get more done than ever before."

—Brian Tracy, author, *How the Best Leaders Lead*

"A masterful and heartfelt exploration of what it means to be an Intelligent Leader. John Mattone guides us through the seven essential traits of a contemporary leader's inner journey, taking the reader deep into the core strength of vulnerability—one of the book's fascinating paradoxes—toward inspired action, self-fulfillment, and creating a lasting legacy. The tone is personal, rich with experience, and authentic. An essential book for our times."

—David Clive Price, author, *Bamboo Strong* and *The Age of Pluralism*

"With so many books coming out on leadership every year, it's rare to read one that brings something truly new and unique to the table. *The Intelligent Leader* does just that. Mattone combines a deep exploration into the heart of what makes great leaders great, with a practical guide that anyone can use to unlock their own potential. It's a must-read for anyone who wants to become a better leader—and human being."

—Dan Hoeyer, founder and CEO, LeadersExcellence

"As an entrepreneur, I've found developing my leadership capacities to be one of the biggest—and most fulfilling—challenges I've faced. John's wisdom and guidance have been invaluable to that process, and his latest book illustrates why. Like few others I've read, this book gets to the authentic heart of the leadership journey—its difficulties and rewards—and gives the reader an intelligent perspective and path to discovering what it looks like to lead in their own unique life and career."

—Rohit Mehrotra, founder, Active Cyber

"John Mattone once again provides a very fresh perspective on leadership, and as he always does, making it practical, actionable, and learnable. His new book shows how true leadership starts from the inside. It gets to the heart of leadership!"

—Tiger Tyagarajan, CEO, Genpact

"John Mattone has evolved his Intelligent Leadership model to manifest this very complete step-by-step manifesto on how you can nurture your core leadership to drive measurable results while enjoying life and work in the process… Wow!"

—Arthur Carmazzi, author, *6 Dimensions of Top Achievers*;
founder, DC Psychology

"John Mattone has done it again. In his new book, he lays out a framework and guide for cultivating and realizing your full leadership potential. Using his seven dimensions of Intelligent Leadership, John helps you bridge your inner core (your character, values, and mindset) with your outer core (your personality, skills, and competencies). This bridge will help you transcend your current level of leadership and reach new levels of influence and impact, all while creating your legacy. Doing this deep work will help you unleash your personal version of the 'X factor' of leadership."

—JD Meier, author, *Getting Results the Agile Way*

"We are living in dramatic times where machine intelligence is challenging human intelligence. John Mattone highlights seven key leadership practices for intelligent leaders to make a difference. This is a must-read book for leaders looking for the right mind-set to get ahead in the artificial intelligence era."

—Alper Utku, president, European Leadership University

"John Mattone has, for years, been developing the most relevant executive coaching techniques. CEO's, corporate leaders, and politicians have sought his counsel to refine their skills as valued assets in the boardroom and community. His extensive knowledge in this field has culminated in this latest work. I highly recommend this book for those looking to develop a competitive edge to pave the road for success."

—Dr. Donovan Essen, DDS, MBA, founder, Essen Dentistry

"John touched the hearts and minds of over 3000 attendees at our 2019 Pendulum Summit in Dublin with his passionate delivery and authenticity, bringing his A game to the stage. He's done it again with his new book! It is a must-read for any person who wants to discover the pathway to achieving more and living a more enriched life—and, who doesn't want that?"

—Frankie Sheahan, founder and CEO, Pendulum Summit

"John is a highly regarded authority on the topic of leadership and his new book is an excellent resource for leaders wishing to step up their game. It distills the wisdom and know-how he has accumulated through the years into an elegant and straightforward read. *The Intelligent Leader* is buzzing with his energy and contains many transformational lessons.

John takes the reader on a journey of self-discovery to uncover the leader within. He is honest and open about the challenges of becoming an exemplary leader in an exacting world. Yet the reader is left with no doubt that the seven secrets he espouses work in the real world and are applicable for exemplary leaders of the future."

—Dr. Peter Chee, president and CEO, ITD World

"If you want to lead others more effectively, John Mattone's book, *The Intelligent Leader*, is a must-have."

—Brenda Bence, author, *Would YOU Want to Work for YOU?*

"*The Intelligent Leader* hits at the core of executive development. In his latest book, John Mattone provides a game plan for executives throughout the world to enhance the way they lead. His approach challenges leaders to make their development a priority so that their culture will thrive as they continually enhance their leadership toolbox. This book should be required reading for executives at all levels who want to lead their teams to success."

—Bryan Powell, PCC Executive Coach and director at Merrill Lynch

"As you read *The Intelligent Leader*, if you're a seasoned leader, you may find yourself frequently saying, like I did, 'John, why didn't you write this book years ago; I would have had greater success and a much more fulfilling career!' If you're new to leadership, you should study, embrace, and live *The Intelligent Leader*. John explores the interplay between our inner core and our outer core through the seven dimensions of Intelligent Leadership, creating an incredibly clear path for you to become your greatest as an individual, while inspiring greatness in those around you. *The Intelligent Leader* is not simply a book on business leadership, it is a guide on personal transformation that transcends cultures, generations, and professions. We are challenged and then taught how to discover the gifts and strengths we have within ourselves—that may have been hidden to us our entire lives—and use them to create the most positive impact in our world."

—Susan Ryan, Master Certified Intelligent Leadership Coach

"John Mattone is one of the world's most respected leadership gurus and he shares his wisdom in this beautiful book. John provides an insightful and compelling framework for leaders trying to navigate the challenges and triumphs of leadership. This book is such an interesting and enjoyable read that you might not notice how much you're learning. Whether you're already in a leadership role or you are an aspiring leader, you will find a wealth of fresh insights, approaches, and practical advice as you learn the seven secrets that will help you become a better leader and a better person."

—Chester Elton, co-author, *All In, The Carrot Principle*, and *The Best Team Wins*

"My singular and most unfortunate regret is meeting my cousin John and his extraordinary talent too late! This latest book, in particular, would have helped me to attain my accomplishments in finance and real estate *immensely* much faster. Nevertheless, we both agree it's never too late."

—Joseph Mattone, chairman, Mattone Group, LLC

"In an era when leaders need to develop an ability to integrate the complexity of the outside world with an understanding of the intricacies of the human inner landscape, John Mattone offers a remarkable tool to explore the different dimensions leaders need to embody to address the defining challenges of our time. *The Intelligent Leader* is a must-read for anyone who wants to understand and experience the inner world of leadership."

—Barbara Dalle Pezze, PhD, Intelligent Leadership
Master Certified Coach and author

"Masterfully written from the heart, this book is a must-read for leaders who are willing to be vulnerable, seeking a breakthrough in their potential, and on a hunt to become the person they must become. I intend to include this book as a key part of the curriculum for emerging leaders as part of Loyola University Maryland's Leadership Essentials Program."

—Lori Raggio, president, Inspire Greatness Coaching and Consulting, LLC

"Mattone has created a leadership book that will be used by generations to come. No matter where in the world you live or work this book will be your go-to guide."

—Nick Roud, executive coach

"*The Intelligent Leader* is without a doubt the go-to guide for those at the high point of their careers as well as those just embarking on their leadership journey. John really highlights the importance of leaving your legacy that will empower all leaders to rethink their primary aim and focus."

—Terry Powell, founder, The Entrepreneur's Source

"Leaders are the individuals within their organizations and communities who have the farthest reach, most impact, a great degree of influence, and the ability to drive culture. And John Mattone's new book, *"The Intelligent Leader,"* is a world-class resource that defines the road map and emotional blueprint for any leader to be successful, regardless of the business or industry they are in! This is a must-read for any leader, at any stage, who wants to tap into and unlock their true potential!"

—Dr. Mike Smith, CEO, Smith Research & Development, LLC

"John Mattone knows what great leadership is. His newest book provides a road map for anyone who chooses the journey to become a better leader. This book provides a process, compelling examples, exercises, and igniter behaviors for how we can improve ourselves and make a bigger impact for all—the organizations we work in, the networks we participate in, and our families and friends. If you want to be a better leader, simply defined as an example for others to follow, then read *The Intelligent Leader* and chart your path to a bigger future."

—Lance Hazzard, author, *Accelerating Leadership*

"Mattone's seven dimensions of Intelligent Leadership inspire Entrepreneurs to lead the future in a practical way with clear vision through examples. I personally encourage Entrepreneurs to read this book many times."

—Hytham El Saiid, founder and CEO, Crowze

"When it comes to leadership, there is always a debate about whether its naturally intuitive or acquired by practice. Hence, it can be developed and improved. Mr. Mattone reveals attractively the methods of effective leadershipthrough a great mixture between passion and realism. His book is a must read, for all kinds of leaders from different fields."

—Sara Al Adba, director, Qatar First Bank

"What struck me most about this book is the care and authenticity that John brings to the realm of leadership development. The insights he shares are ones that he has worked hard for—throughout his personal and professional career—and he presents them in a way that is relatable (and actionable) to anyone who wants to become more or better. These are truly gems of wisdom gleaned from John's life and the lives of the many great leaders he's worked with over the years."

—Rashid Mohammed Al Naimi, CEO, Doha Business Solutions

"This remarkable book will teach you what true leadership feels like from the inside out and what you need to do to get to where you want to go. You'll learn the dynamics of the human heart, mind, and soul—including your own. Destined to become a leadership classic!"

—Jason Jennings, author, *The Reinventors* and *Think BIG, Act Small*

"Before you take the next step on your journey to exemplary leadership, pack a copy of John Mattone's brilliant new book *The Intelligent Leader*. It is an essential guide to exploring the most important question every leader must answer: Who are you and who do you want to become? *The Intelligent Leader* is a refreshing, rare, and wise book that espouses some too-often overlooked vital qualities of leadership—qualities such as vulnerability, duty, and humility. It is also a practical book chocked full of engaging examples and useful action steps. *The Intelligent Leader* will inspire you, encourage you, and enlighten you. I highly recommend that you take to heart Mattone's sage advice and counsel."

—Jim Kouzes, co-author, *The Leadership Challenge*;
Executive Fellow, Leavey School of Business

"John Mattone cuts to the chase and gets to the roots of high performance and effective leadership. It all starts with growing and maturing your Inner Core. In his new book, Mattone shares the wisdom that comes from a career spent coaching and mentoring CEOs of Fortune 500 companies, including Steve Jobs. He is not content with sharing some quick fix, or some smart skills. He knows that unless you do the inner work, your results will not be consistent and you will not develop and express your greatest potential into the world. This book gives you access to the essence of great leadership, whether you are at the top of your career or just at the beginning. He does so in an engaging, convincing, and deep way. This is essential reading, if you are committed to leave a dent in the universe and experience fulfillment in your career and life."

—Aldo Civico, executive coach

"Becoming a good leader is possible. It is not a quality reserved for a few. I have always been surprised by the ease with which John helps people to develop their leadership skills. With *The Intelligent Leader*, John has outdone himself. It is a brilliant and simple guide based on seven very powerful secrets that are necessary to become a good leader–an intelligent leader. This book is inspirational and guides you through a soul search on a voyage to leadership"

—Armando Uriegas, president, LatAm Zone, Nielson

"*The Intelligent Leader* is like a report from the frontlines of the effort to unlock our human potential, and John Mattone is the seasoned correspondent who is sharing everything he's learned. This book is comprehensive, authentic, practical, and often-moving. I highly recommend it for anyone who wants to be a better example for others to follow."
—Kate Sweetman, founding principal, SweetmanCragun Group; co-author, *Reinvention: Accelerating Results in the Age of Disruption*

"John Mattone has advised some of the world's most influential leaders. In his new book, he shares his latest thought-provoking and heartfelt insights on how to become a better leader and positively impact the lives of others in order to create a better future for generations to come."
—Christopher G. Lis, former president and COO, Lexington Health Network

"Don't be fooled by all of the hyperbolic and 'quick tip' advice for leadership success. Great leadership starts and ends with a good, hard look in the mirror and a willingness to do what it takes to improve—for your own sake and for the sake of those around you. That's what Intelligent Leadership is all about. This book will take you as far (and as deep) as you want to go."
—Sheikha Kaltham Al Thani, head of business application and systems, Qatar Development Bank

"So many people think they want to be leaders, but few do what it takes to succeed. *The Intelligent Leader* is a perfect guidebook for those who want to do the inner work and take the kind of responsibility required to lead and inspire others."
—Prof. Ibrahim Alnaimi, undersecretary, Ministry of Education and Higher Education, Qatar

"This book is for existing and aspiring leaders, laying out a subtle-yet-simple path that anyone can take to be the kind of person that inspires others to follow their lead. John Mattone's guided philosophy with real-world examples unlocks potential of great leadership values."
—H.E. Dr. Rania Al Mashat, Minister of Tourism, Arab Republic of Egypt

"Few people understand the essence of the leadership journey as well as John Mattone. He is a master of helping you see directly in your own life where your opportunities to grow lie, and how to pursue that growth. This book should be required reading for every MBA student in the US and the World."
—Vegar Wiik, Executive Director, College of Business, Florida Atlantic University

THE
INTELLIGENT LEADER

UNLOCKING THE
7 SECRETS TO
LEADING OTHERS
AND LEAVING
YOUR LEGACY

JOHN MATTONE

WILEY

Library of Congress Cataloging-in-Publication Data:

Names: Mattone, John, author.
Title: The intelligent leader : unlocking the 7 secrets to leading others and leaving your legacy / John Mattone.
Description: First Edition. | Hoboken : Wiley, 2020. | Includes index.
Identifiers: LCCN 2019024555 (print) | LCCN 2019024556 (ebook) | ISBN 9781119566243 (hardback) | ISBN 9781119566328 (adobe pdf) | ISBN 9781119566335 (epub)
Subjects: LCSH: Leadership. | Executive ability.
Classification: LCC HD57.7 .M3932 2019 (print) | LCC HD57.7 (ebook) | DDC 658.4/092--dc23
LC record available at https://lccn.loc.gov/2019024555
LC ebook record available at https://lccn.loc.gov/2019024556

Printed in the United States of America
V10013410_082719

To Marshall, for all that you have brought to the world of coaching, leadership, and beyond, and for being a tremendous inspiration to me.

Contents

Foreword

Whether you're an established executive or manager looking to take your leadership game to the next level, or someone looking to move into a position of leadership in the future, you'll find no better guide for your journey than John Mattone. John is one of the most respected executive coaches in the world and a pioneer in leadership development. He has helped some of the world's most influential leaders to unlock their own potential. And he can do the same for you, if you let him.

What makes John's approach to leadership development so unique—and powerful—is his emphasis on what he calls the "inner core," which is a new term for good old-fashioned things like character, values, and beliefs. He is steadfast in his belief that truly great leadership starts on the inside and works its way out. It takes courage. It takes vulnerability. And it takes heart. Leadership isn't just a sexy set of techniques or inspiring ideas. It's the product of deep work that you forge at the level of your heart and soul.

The Intelligent Leader may be John's most important work to date. In it, he distills the work he's done with thousands of clients over the years into an accessible, warm, and intimate exploration into what it takes to lead, empower, and inspire others. The book lays out his Seven Dimensions of Intelligent Leadership, which are both the universal qualities of great leadership as well as actionable principles that you can use to evolve yourself. While John's work is inspired by his work with business executives, this isn't just a business book. As John makes clear, we all have leadership potential within us and cultivating it will help us to lead more influential, fulfilling, and enriching lives.

As you embark on your journey into the book, one bit of advice: Remember that change is hard. It often takes longer than you think, and it can be difficult. Don't just read John's book; put it into practice. Pick up the tools he offers, and take personal ownership of your success. Remember, real change is not a one-time thing, and it requires real effort. Being an authentic leader, both inside and out, is a lifetime pursuit!

Life is good.
Marshall Goldsmith

Preface: A Demand for Depth

Since 2013, when I published *Intelligent Leadership*, a lot has changed—in my own life and career, and in the world. Personally, I am honored to have witnessed an explosion of interest in my work, specifically the Intelligent Leadership model. I've worked with companies—big and small—and executives—famous and unknown—on nearly every continent. I've spoken at conferences and in boardrooms. I've even been named one of the world's top executive coaches. I don't bring this up to brag about my success or to impress you. I truly mean that. To me, the growing popularity of my work is a statement less about me personally, and more about the state of leadership in the world today.

One of the things that makes Intelligent Leadership (IL) unique—the true secret of IL—is the emphasis it puts on the inner work required to develop your leadership capacities. I've found that in order to achieve the results that most leaders are after—improved performance, career advancement, personal and company success, and leaving a lasting legacy—leaders must be willing to find the courage to "look under the hood" and start to understand just what it is that makes them tick. Then everyone must do the work to unleash their inner light so that it shines through to every dimension of their lives. We will be exploring this in great depth throughout the coming pages.

I've found that this depth approach is, for the most part, missing in leadership circles today. Many people either don't take the appropriate time, or don't have the knowledge or interest, to seriously explore their interiors. They tend to skip over all of that in order to get to the quick, easy, results-oriented stuff. But in doing so, they ignore the crucial value that this kind of self-knowledge has on your ability to lead. The great leaders that I've met all know this. It is, I believe, what makes them great.

To be honest, I think this demand for depth is at the heart of the "leadership gap" that so many people have written about over the past couple of decades. Members of an entire generation of leaders, people my age (I'm sixty-two) and older, haven't put a sufficient emphasis on getting to know themselves, and for good reason. They've been primarily focused on building and growing companies, getting the job done, and delivering results to the many people who depend on them. Many of these great men and women have learned their leadership lessons through a lifetime of experience, but haven't necessarily had the language or the tools to pass on to the next generation what they themselves understand implicitly. The aspiring leaders of today, Gen X and Gen Y, are much more open to the kind of inner work that's at the core of IL, but they don't have teachers to teach them. There aren't enough roadmaps out there for potential leaders to prepare themselves, at the level of the heart, mind, and soul, for what great leadership really entails.

That is why I wanted to write this book. *The Intelligent Leader* is meant to be a roadmap for understanding the true essence of the leadership journey. My first IL book was an attempt to introduce the world to the work I've been doing to integrate the enneagram into a leadership tool that I call the Mattone Leadership Enneagram Inventory (MLEI). It was full of workbooks and activities to help you explore your unique strengths and weaknesses as a human being and a leader. It's been very useful to many people. But since the publication of that book, new principles have emerged in my work. I've started to see patterns emerge in the many leaders I've worked with, and from those patterns, I believe I'm starting to see the picture of the true essence of great leadership, both how it feels on the inside and how it looks from the outside.

In *The Intelligent Leader,* I will share all of that with you, the reader. It is meant to guide you on a journey into the heart of leadership, exploring its many dimensions, and then stand with you as you peer back out, through your soul and personality, to see what the world looks like from that new vantage point. If I achieve my goal with this book, it will give you a direct experience of what truly great leadership feels like, from the inside out, so that you have a sense of what you're shooting for, and what you need to do to get there.

The world today needs leaders to have this new kind of intelligence. They need to understand the subtle dynamics of the human heart, mind, and soul, starting with their own. They need to be rooted in powerful self-knowledge and to cultivate a rare but achievable ability to bring about the same rootedness in those around them. You could call it Enlightened Leadership, or Deep Leadership, but I prefer "Intelligent." It speaks to just how savvy you can become if you put in the time to learn this approach.

I truly believe that this kind of Intelligent Leadership is not a luxury but a requirement for leaders today. And it's my honor to share with you what I consider to be the secrets to becoming the great leader you have the potential to be.

Acknowledgments

This book, like my other books, required the commitment, sacrifice, and hard work of many.

I want to thank my incredible wife of forty-one years, Gayle, who has stood by me every step of the way. Gayle is the most courageous individual I have ever known. She is a two-time breast cancer survivor who never gave up on life, who persevered and continues to persevere to help others through her work as a senior registered nurse at the University of Central Florida. Gayle is a remarkable role model for our entire family and the world. Gayle, I love you.

Our four children and their loved ones—Jared, Nicholas, Kristina and Darrin, and Matthew and Cassee—and our four grandchildren—Luke Dominic Mattone, Dylan John DiBisceglie, Easton Matthew Mattone, and Ava Lorraine DiBisceglie. Your love is my strength. I love you. I want to thank my late parents, Dominic and Jane Mattone, and my late father- and mother-in-law, Bill and Jean O'Halloran. We are comforted and strengthened knowing that you look down upon us each and every day. We go forward every day with pride, honor, and confidence beneath our wings.

I want to thank all my clients who have attended my speeches, executive retreats, workshops, and programs, and those whom I have had the privilege to coach and consult with throughout the years. I have learned so much from you, and I thank you for your contributions to this book. I especially want to thank my close advisor and friend, Joel Pitney, who worked tirelessly with me for well over a year on this book. Thank you, Joel, for your wisdom, creativity, and for your undying commitment to me and this project.

I'd also like to thank his wife, Laura Pitney, whose careful editing helped bring the manuscript to the next level.

I want to thank my incredible team at John Mattone Global, Inc.: my sons Nicholas Mattone, our Chief Relationship Officer, and Matthew Mattone, our Chief Operations Officer; Trevor Maloney, our Chief Development Officer; and Sean Ryan, our Chief Strategy Officer. I'd like to thank our marketing team, led by Manny Janero, Gonzalo Montes de Oca, and Launch My Book, Inc.; our finance and administrative team, led by Lauryn Charles, Kristina DiBisceglie, and Cassee Zopp; and our legal counsel, Jeffrey Garber, Esq., and Carl Spagnuolo, Esq. Thank you to our friend, colleague, and advisor Paul Cortissoz.

I want to thank our outstanding training team: Susan Ryan, our Director of IL Advanced Training and Master IL Trainer; Kalpana Shanmugham, PhD, Master IL Trainer; and Lori Raggio, Master IL Trainer. I would like to thank our over 450 certified Intelligent Leadership (IL) Executive Coaches who represent 52 different countries around the world. I would like to extend a special thanks to my friend Terry Powell, founder of Franchise Source Brands, the Entrepreneurs Source, and AdviCoach Franchise, who shared my vision for co-creating and launching the AdviCoach-Intelligent Leadership Coaching Franchise Brand to provide entrepreneurial opportunities to leaders all over the world who want to start and grow their own coaching firms.

I want to thank our friend, colleague, and valued business partner Monir Fady of Doha Business Solutions (DBS) and the DBS leadership team for their support of my work throughout the Middle East, Europe, and Africa. I want to thank Taha Farhan and the team from Global Gurus for their support, and I want to extend a special thanks to Des Dearlove and Stuart Crainer from the Thinkers50 for their belief in me and my work. And, of course, I want to thank all our event partners and global speaker bureau partners for their support as well.

I want to extend a special thank you to my friends and colleagues at the University of Central Florida (UCF): Dr. Michael

Johnson, Dean of the College of Sciences; Dr. Florian Jentsch, Chair, Department of Psychology; Dr. Steven Jex, Director of the Ph.D. Program in Industrial/Organizational Psychology; Dr. Victoria Pace, Director of the Master's Program in I/O Psychology; and Millie Erichsen, Senior Director of Advancement, Department of Sciences. I would like to extend my thanks and appreciation to the Master's and Ph.D. students in I/O Psychology at UCF and to thank all my executive MBA students at Florida Atlantic University. The world of academia and business will only get better as soon as you enter the workforce. You have had great mentors and teachers along the way.

I want to thank my early mentor Dr. Joseph Weintraub, Professor of Management at Babson College, who introduced me to the field of industrial/organizational psychology and who inspired me to continue onto graduate school. I want to thank Dr. Wayne Burroughs, formerly Director of the I/O Psychology Department at UCF, who mentored and challenged me to reach my potential. And I want to thank my first corporate mentor, the late Lou Larsen, who believed in me even more than I believed in myself.

I want to thank my colleagues and friends from AlignMark—Cabot Jaffee Sr., Cabot Jaffee, Glen Jaffee, Mike Struth—for what I learned from you and for providing me the wisdom and passion to do what I do today. I also want to thank Bonnie Hagemann, CEO of Executive Development Associates, and the entire team at EDA for being great business partners.

My acknowledgments would not be complete if I didn't mention those in the field of leadership and coaching who have inspired and had a tremendous impact on me and my career. I begin with Dr. Marshall Goldsmith, to whom I have dedicated this book. I also want to thank Tony Robbins, John Maxwell, Ken Blanchard, and the late Steven Covey for all that you have done to inspire me. There are so many others who have helped me, guided me, coached me—I apologize if I didn't mention you. Thank you for helping me along the way!

Finally, this project would not have been possible without the support of Matthew Holt, publisher, and the outstanding efforts of senior editor Jeanenne Ray and her team at John Wiley & Sons, Inc., as well as the editing of Vicki Adang. Thank you very much for all of your excellent work.

Introduction: Do You Have What It Takes to Inspire Others to Follow?

When you think of the word "leader," what comes to mind? You might imagine someone powerful or inspiring. It could be a person who always seems to be one step ahead of others. You may think of someone specific—someone famous, or someone you know personally. You may even think of yourself.

The truth is, leadership can take many forms, and can look many different ways. Yet finding a *true* leader is like coming across a rare gem—it doesn't happen every day. You see, while the idea of *being* a leader excites folks, often they're actually only interested in what it will do for them. Perhaps they want power, control, wealth, accolades, or improved status. But the true leaders I've encountered in my life are those who view leadership not as a benefit to themselves, but as an obligation to others.

That's why my favorite definition of leadership, which you can read right there in the dictionary, is this: "an example for others to follow." A defining characteristic of some of the greatest leaders I've had the privilege of knowing is that they design their lives according to an obligation to others. They're aware that people around them are depending on them and modeling their lives after them. Accordingly, these leaders strive to become better people. This is the unsexy secret of becoming a truly great leader—and honestly, there aren't many people willing to take on such enormous responsibility. I think this is one of the primary root causes of the leadership gap so many people are talking about in the business world these days.

But I don't mean to paint a dismal picture or discourage you. I actually see the challenge of becoming a great leader as a profound opportunity. The best leaders aren't necessarily those who are born with some special "gift." They've made a decision to take on the enormous responsibility of becoming an example for others—and you can too. Anyone can. Assuming the mantle of leadership is a choice anyone can make. Great leadership is a skill you can develop. That's what "Intelligent Leadership" is all about.

If you're someone who truly wants to evolve as a leader, and you're comfortable with becoming "an example for others to follow," then this book will show you a pathway to do so. It's based on research, both formal and informal, that I've conducted over decades as an industrial psychologist and leadership coach. I've worked with some of the best leaders in the business world—some famous, others relatively unknown—and I've developed an approach to leadership that anyone can use to become a truly great leader—and human being.

We'll go into great detail about Intelligent Leadership in the chapters that follow, but first I want to explore just what "great leadership" looks like.

IDENTIFYING THE GOAL

When you're trying to achieve something, it's important to have as clear a picture of your goal as possible. So before we go any further, I want to do a little exercise with you: Envision two different people who you consider to be great examples of leadership. One of those leaders should be someone famous: a Martin Luther King, Jr. or a Ronald Reagan or a Sheryl Sandberg-type character who, to you, best embodies the true essence of leadership. Your second example should be someone from your own life. It could be a boss, a mentor, teacher, pastor, coach, or parent. Choose someone who has been an example you've followed in your life and who has inspired you to do more, or to be better.

Now that you have your two examples in mind, I'd like you to think about what *makes* each one a great leader. What are the qualities, characteristics, and capacities they embody that inspire others? Be as specific as you can.

Examples that come to my mind include the late Steve Jobs, a former client of mine, who was an innovator and trendsetter. He always seemed to be at least two steps ahead of everyone else. I think of the pioneer Amelia Earhart, who wasn't afraid to do things no one before her had ever done. My old baseball coach, who was unwilling to allow any of his players to settle for anything less than their best, continues to inspire me. I think of great athletes, like Lebron James or Alex Morgan, who are so personally dedicated to consistent improvement that they inspire others to do the same.

Now, go ahead and make a list of two individuals and their leadership qualities, and keep it handy. We'll use it for reference as we move through the book.

THE X FACTOR

I'm going to go out on a limb here and assume that, in addition to the qualities you listed, both of the leaders you thought of have an indefinable quality, something about each of them that can't easily be articulated. This is a kind of "X factor" beyond their specific attributes giving them an extra leadership glow—a seemingly irreducible quality that's difficult to point to, yet powerfully present in the greatest leaders.

This elusive quality contributes to the false assumption that people are born as great leaders—that they have a God-given talent for inspiring others that just seems to flow naturally from the core of who they are. And while I do believe that some people are "born leaders," I've also come to believe, through countless experiences, that this leadership quality isn't necessarily something you're born with. It can be developed. You may never shine as brightly as Nelson Mandela or Bill Gates, but you can significantly evolve your own ability to be an example to others, and that's what we're going to spend the rest of this book learning how to do.

In my experience, this "X factor" of great leadership comes from cultivating a powerful connection to what I call your "inner core." We're going to spend a lot of time defining the inner core in the next chapter, but for now let's use the metaphor of an iceberg. If you visualize an iceberg, you can see the white or blue ice towering above the waterline. But below the surface, what you can't see, is a giant mass that makes up the vast majority of the iceberg, and that accounts for its movements through the ocean. So, like that iceberg, your inner core is everything in you that lies below the surface, all the "invisible" qualities that anchor your personality and that result in the skills and actions that people see.

Now, not everyone describes the inner core in this manner. Theologians and psychologists, and people far more intelligent than I from various disciplines and philosophical orientations, have different definitions for the inner core, whether it be the soul, the spirit, or the subconscious. To me, one's inner core is the combination of self-concept, character, and values that, together, most deeply influences how we move through and respond to the world.

The greatest leaders, in my experience, are those who are not only deeply aware of their inner terrain, but also skilled at accessing it, changing it, and using it to guide and shape their actions in the world. Their connection to their inner core is the "glow" of great leadership. It's the indefinable quality that makes great people tick.

The Intelligent Leadership (IL) model is designed to help you zero in on and cultivate your inner core so that you can start to exude the X Factor of great leadership. It may sound grandiose, but IL essentially breaks down the mysterious and often elusive qualities of great leadership and shows you, very practically, how to improve them in your own mind, heart, and soul. It essentially "reduces the irreducible" and gives you a concrete framework and blueprint for leadership development.

The Leadership Gap

There is a tremendous amount of intellectual power in the corporate world today. I've sat in boardrooms of some of the world's biggest companies, and I'm awestruck by the sheer intelligence and cognitive capacities of those surrounding me. Companies have done a very good job of finding and cultivating their intellectual capital. And yet, in spite of all that, study after study and book after book find the same thing: there's a lack of strong leadership in virtually every industry.

What does this tell us? I see a simple but often difficult to perceive truth: good leadership requires something more than just intellectual power. If you were to chart the intellectual and leadership abilities of most companies, like in Figure I.1, you'd see a skewed bell curve. The Y-axis represents the number of leaders, and the X-axis represents their capacities. As you can see, there are more leaders with high levels of cognitive capacity (represented by the curve on the right) than there are leaders with high levels of leadership capacity (represented by the curve on the left).

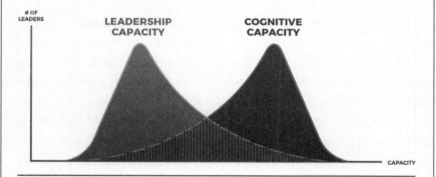

FIGURE I.1   The Leadership Gap.

So why the gap? Why are there more leaders with high levels of intellect than there are leaders who possess a high degree of leadership strength? What's missing? That's what this book is all about. In order to translate intellectual power into strong leadership ability, you need to tap into the invisible elements of your inner core.

THE WHOLE ENCHILADA

Now, before you think that this book is going to go "soft" and focus only on the hard-to-define subjective qualities of the "inner core," I want to stop you right there. The whole point of the Intelligent Leadership process is to drive real, measurable results. In fact, one of the things that makes this unique amidst the panoply of leadership development techniques and philosophies on the market today is the way it combines an appreciation for both the inner core elements and the "outer core" capacities that drive your performance in the real world.

There are literally thousands of new leadership books published every year, and most of them tend to skew in one direction or the other. Some focus primarily on the subjective, inner experience of the individual; these tend to lack accountability or direct connections to how this inner work can translate into improved performance. Others try to skip over the important inner work that I've found is required to make real, sustained change in our "outer" capacities a reality.

I say that it's *all* important. Unless you're giving equal weight to both your inner core and your outer competencies, then you're not going to develop in significant ways. Intelligent Leadership, which is made up of seven dimensions that we'll spend the good majority of this book exploring, is the key to unlocking this powerful connection between the inner and the outer, the subjective and the objective, the invisible world below the surface and the visible qualities and capacities that make us great leaders.

WE'RE ALL LEADERS

So who should read this book? My short answer is: anyone who wants to become a better human being.

One of my pet peeves is that many people have an unconscious assumption about who is and isn't a leader. People in leadership circles tend to ascribe a lot of significance to titles and positions, which I've found can sometimes get in the way of the real essence of leadership development. In fact, if you read some of my previous books, you'll see that I have, to a degree, succumbed to that same assumption. Much of what I've published in the past has been very specifically focused on helping people who are in formal positions of leadership in the business world—managers, VPs, CEOs—to become more effective.

The truth is that in the work I've done with thousands of people over the years, I've found that the principles driving great leadership are similar, if not identical, to the principles that drive any realm of human development. At the end of the day, what is a good leader if not a good *human*? Remember, the definition we're using for leadership is "being an example for others to follow." And who isn't an example to *someone*? Even if you're not in a position of formal leadership, you're probably a parent, a coach, a teacher, or simply a friend.

Just by getting out of bed in the morning and entering the complex world of human relationships, you have influence on others. You're an example of something to someone, whether you like it or not. And we all have room to change and improve the kind of example we are.

THE ROAD AHEAD

In the first chapter of this book, we'll take a deep dive into the complex relationship between your inner core and your outer capacities for leadership. We'll explore the many practical ways that focusing on your inner core will provide the foundation for your outer capacities to flourish and shine. We'll talk about the developmental process itself, and how best to approach the inner and outer work we'll be doing together.

Once we've established a baseline understanding of how the inner and outer core work together to unlock your leadership potential, we'll spend the next seven chapters exploring the key elements of Intelligent Leadership. We'll define these seven principles using stories, models, and examples, and give you concrete actions you can take to develop in regard to each. This will be the core of the book and the key to mastering the art of Intelligent Leadership.

We'll then complete our journey together with an exploration of the subtle and important connection between leadership and culture. We'll talk about the direct ways that your development as a leader can help to influence the culture of your team, your employees, your workplace, your family, and I'll show you how to translate IL to the people around you.

ESTABLISHING YOUR NETWORK

One of the most important elements of Intelligent Leadership is the use of feedback from others to help you identify your strengths and weaknesses, and to help track your developmental progress. Before we dive into the meat of the book, I'd like you to identify a few key people you can count on for feedback. Ideally, you want to select people you trust will be honest—a friend, co-worker, boss, employee, spouse. In each chapter of the book, I'll ask you to reach out to your network to give you reflections on how they perceive you in relationship to the particular dimension we're discussing. This information will be absolutely invaluable. Their feedback will not only give you an accurate sense of what you need to work on, but also confidence that you're developing!

AN INVITATION TO GO DEEP

I have confidence in the power of Intelligent Leadership to transform those individuals who take it seriously. I don't mean this to be self-congratulatory. The IL dimensions are something that I've *discovered* through my work with thousands of leaders and aspiring leaders. Some days I feel like an archaeologist of the human mind, heart, and soul, discovering new patterns in the geology of leadership through every interview, coaching session, or interaction I have. This book is where I'm publishing my discoveries—the code for leadership transformation that I've uncovered.

I invite you to open your heart and mind as much as you can as you read and work through this book. "Going deep" and exploring the subtle territory of your inner core can be a difficult experience. It requires vulnerability. It requires courage. It requires a kind of inner strength that we all have inside of us if we choose to exercise it. I guarantee that it will be worth your effort. I've seen too many success stories to think otherwise.

CHAPTER 1

Getting to Know Thyself

If you've ever taken an introductory philosophy class or spent any time reading the wide variety of personal development books available today, you've probably run across the phrase "Know thyself." This ancient Greek aphorism was popularized by Socrates, who, according to his pupil Plato, expanded upon it to make the famous claim "An unexamined life is not worth living."

I bring this up not to bore you with a review of the history of Western philosophy, but to orient you to the kind of inquiry that lies at the heart of Intelligent Leadership. If you want to develop as a leader, which means developing as a human being, it's crucial that you examine yourself as deeply as you can. You need to understand what drives you, what tends to get in the way of your success, and what latent gifts you might possess.

As we discussed in the introduction, the key to making sure your self-inquiry leads to real, lasting results is knowing *what* you're examining. Are you looking primarily at accomplishments, skills, and behaviors (the part of the iceberg that's above the surface—the outer core)? Or are you examining the deeper structures of your inner core, which comprises character, values, thinking patterns, and beliefs? The Intelligent Leadership model is focused on developing your knowledge of all these dimensions of yourself. More specifically, the IL helps you to understand the relationship between your inner and outer core.

I love models. They help us to visualize the invisible structures that make up the subjective dimensions of who we are. Figure 1.1 is the model that I've developed to illustrate the relationship between our inner and outer core that is at the heart of transforming our mindset. The model represents the sum total of who we are and, like an onion, has layers. The deepest layer is our "inner

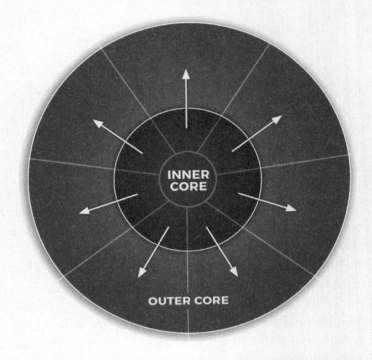

FIGURE 1.1   The relationship between the inner and outer core.

core"—our character and values, our thinking patterns and beliefs. The inner core has its own layers, which we'll explore further below. The surface layer of the model is what the world sees in us: our personality, behavior, skills, and capabilities.

Now let's explore the model in more detail, starting with the inner core.

GETTING TO THE WHY OF THINGS

So what exactly is the inner core? This is a very good question, and a very difficult one to answer. The inner core is fundamental to who we are, and yet it is completely invisible to us most of the time. I like to think of it as the "why" of everything we do. It's a kind of blueprint, constructed by our upbringing, life choices, and experience, that shapes our lives and determines the kind of person we are.

While the inner core is, in its essence, very difficult to define, I've dedicated much of my career to understanding and measuring its influence in leaders all over the world. And I've broken it down into four primary components: your character, your values, your self-concept, and your beliefs.

Let's start with character. The word "character" is usually used to describe the moral qualities of an individual. Someone with character possesses a kind of integrity or inner strength that reverberates through every aspect of who they are. One of the best definitions of character I've ever encountered came from an unlikely place: an eighth grader I met while giving a talk at a middle school in Orlando, where I live.

A close friend, Judy, is the principal of the school and had asked me to address their 500 graduating eighth graders along with their parents, grandparents, and friends—about 2,000 people in all. Judy wanted me to speak to the young graduates primarily about the importance of character for leadership and success. Following a wonderful introduction by Judy, I stood before the 500 graduates and posed the question, "Does anyone want to propose a great definition of character?"

After three or four seconds, a young man put his hand up. I called on him and he softly muttered some powerful words that only a few of his classmates and I could hear. His words so impressed me that I asked him his name and he said, "Amant." I then asked him if he would share his definition with everyone (this time using the microphone). "Yes," he replied.

"Parents, grandparents, friends, everyone," I announced, "Amant would like to share his definition of character." With that, I turned the microphone over to him. Amant stood up and with pride and eloquence, stated, "Character is what you do when no one else is watching." The crowd erupted in applause. I was awestruck, not because I had never heard this definition, but rather because of Amant's clarity and conviction in sharing this powerful

definition. It moved me and the thousands of people in atten-
dance. Clearly, this young man recognized the value of possessing
a working definition of character as a guide to his everyday decision making.

HOW STRONG IS YOUR CHARACTER?

In the spirit of Amant, I'd like you to take a moment and consider
who *you* are when no one else is watching. In what ways do you
exhibit strong character? Are there ways in which you are lacking
character? Again, this may feel like an unfamiliar exercise for you,
but it's the key to unlocking your leadership potential.

To help you with your inquiry, I'll provide you with some criteria for assessing your character. I define character as having six
elements, which I've outlined below. They are quite literally the
map of your character, which is an essential component of your
inner core. As you read through them, consider how strongly you
exhibit each element and where you might have room to grow. See
if you can see any patterns emerging.

Courage

When you think of courage, it's easy to imagine some kind of
mythical hero slaying a dragon or rescuing someone from danger.
And while this grandiose version of courage may be inspired by
the essence of the word, the true definition of courage is usually
much more subtle than that. Courage, as a defining trait of character, is simply the willingness to sacrifice oneself for a greater
purpose—whether that be speaking truth to power, risking your
reputation by making a controversial decision, or doing the "right"
thing when there's a tremendous amount of pressure to do otherwise. Courage doesn't mean feeling fearless, but being willing to
act out of conviction in spite of that fear.

Where do you stand in relationship to courage? How willing
are you to sacrifice yourself for others or for what's right?

Loyalty

When I speak about loyalty, I don't mean "blind" loyalty to a person regardless of their actions. Loyalty is literally the glue that holds our relationships together—the fabric of our communities and organizations. Loyalty is what allows us to support one another, through thick and through thin, even when it may not be convenient to do so. Loyalty is not a one-way commitment, but must function both upwardly and downwardly. Loyalty directed upward is the loyalty you show to your superiors, tempered by the assumption that the superiors are lawful and ethical. "Downward" loyalty is about leaders' responsibility to care for their people. It's "loyalty to the troops" and it's every bit as essential as upward loyalty.

Is loyalty important to you? Do you find that you are committed to others, even when it's difficult, and take action on it?

Diligence

Diligence, in its essence, is having the understanding that there are no shortcuts to worthwhile achievements. Anyone settling for the quickest, easiest, shortest way to get an outcome is bound for disappointment. If you're willing to put in the work, to make sure you've done everything you can to succeed, you experience a confidence that can't be shaken. Diligent leaders are much more resilient in the face of setbacks because they are prepared in advance for the inevitability of a bumpy road, and they are able to steer forward despite challenges. They don't have that nagging feeling that they could have done more or been more discerning. Diligence provides a kind of bedrock quality to your character that will allow you to remain steady amidst the chaos of the world around you.

How diligent is your approach to life? Do you avoid cutting corners in order to know that you've done things the right way?

Modesty

Leaders tend to have a tremendous amount of confidence, which makes modesty one of the most important elements of building a strong character. Modesty, at its core, is about living within limits. It is the antithesis of aggressiveness, presumptuousness, and arrogance. The most effective leaders recognize that they are *not* "too big to fail," and they are open to other perspectives in the interest of improving themselves and the organization. To the modest leader, fiscal and operational constraints are safeguards rather than hindrances. Modesty also serves to keep your emotions in balance. If you can recognize that your more arrogant impulses are based in a need for attention, you can cultivate a calmer self-acceptance in the face of challenges.

Would you consider yourself a modest person? Are you able to keep your ambitions in check?

Honesty

It would seem that honesty would be a no-brainer when it comes to character, but the truth is that being an honest person is actually more difficult than one might think. Especially when faced with enormous pressure, it can often be easier to sacrifice the truth in the name of expediency, profit, or personal advancement. The best leaders willingly miss out on deals that would require deception to win. A smaller profit made with honesty is worth more than a bigger profit made dishonestly. Acts of dishonesty—padded expense accounts, shaved tax forms, arriving to work late and leaving early, or theft of company property—accumulate, and create a toxic environment in yourself and your team. On the other hand, a leader with maturity and honesty creates a truthful, above-board environment.

How important is honesty to you? Do you ever sacrifice the truth for the sake of getting something?

Gratitude

While saying thank you and making sure those around you know they are appreciated are important *expressions* of gratitude, when it comes to character, I'm talking about something deeper than that. Gratitude comes from an understanding that there will be highs and lows in our lives, and in any endeavor we take on. Like a batting average, higher is better, but the occasional strikeout can be a learning experience too. In fact, experiencing the lows is what keeps us in balance and lets us appreciate the successes all the more. If you're keeping a bird's-eye view on your life, and don't feel entitled to success, gratitude for what comes your way will be the natural result.

How grateful do you feel in your own life? Are you able to maintain a big perspective about your victories and successes?

As you reviewed and contemplated these six elements of character, did you see any patterns start to emerge? In my experience working with leaders of all types, I find the contemplation of character one of the most revealing exercises. It helps to paint a picture of how much inner strength you tend to have in the face of difficult circumstances, and it shows you some very concrete ways in which you can improve these fundamental elements of who you are.

As important as character is, it's only one part of the inner core equation. The next key component of your inner core is your values. Let's explore.

VALUES: YOUR CRITERIA FOR LIFE

If you want to understand yourself, it's imperative that you start to explore why you do the things you do. This is where your values come in. The word "values" can mean many things. You might think of a specific value like "family" or "success" or "recognition." One of the best definitions of values comes from a friend and colleague of mine—Dr. Aldo Civico, an executive leadership coach and conflict negotiator, who has spent decades working to bring about the highest potential in leaders from around the world. Aldo, like me, loves to define the subtle terrain of our interiors. He describes values as our "criteria for life." Our values, especially our deep-seated ones, are the lens through which we see the world. They are at play in every major decision we make. Some of our values may be principles that we've cultivated ourselves. Others were instilled in us by our parents or by society. Whether we're aware of our values or not, they are informing our every move, and to a significant degree determine our destiny.

And yet, in my experience, very few of us actually take the time to really get clear about what our values are. We tend to simply move through life acting upon values that we've never made conscious in ourselves. And this can often lead to problems.

For example, I've worked with executives who seem to have a very difficult time maintaining strong relationships in their lives, which can hold them back both personally and professionally. After some exploration into their unconscious values, it became clear that they were being driven primarily by a strong value for success and achievement, which was a huge asset in many ways but, when left unchecked, would often conflict with their desire for improving their interactions and bonds with others. It wasn't until we mapped their value set that we were able to identify this discrepancy and therefore begin to shift the balance in their lives.

So in the spirit of self-inquiry, let's take a deeper look into your own value matrix. There are many different kinds of values a person can have, but for the purposes of Intelligent Leadership, we want to focus primarily on what are called "ultimate" values. Ultimate values, like recognition or security, are fundamental to who we are and underlie our more immediate values, like money or family. When trying to get to the bedrock of our values, I like to use the construct of values researched by Drs. Joyce and Robert Hogan and measured by their popular "Hogan Motives, Values, and Interest Survey," It identifies ten ultimate values:

1. *Aesthetics:* Art, literature, culture, imagination
2. *Affiliation:* Social interactions
3. *Altruism:* Desire to serve others, to improve everything
4. *Commercial:* Earning money, realizing profits
5. *Hedonism:* Desire for fun, excitement, variety

6. *Power:* Desire for achievement, competition, getting ahead
7. *Recognition:* Desire to be known, visible, self-display, famous
8. *Science:* Analytical, new ideas, technology
9. *Security:* Structure, predictability, prudence
10. *Tradition:* Appropriate social behavior, morality, high standards

Again, these ultimate values make up the fundamental drivers of who we are and how we act, and have a significant influence on our leadership style. And each of us has a different values matrix. Some of us are driven primarily by power or tradition, while others are more interested in recognition or altruism. Getting to know your own hierarchy of values is an important part of understanding just exactly what it is that makes you tick.

To that end, I'd like you to take some time and rank these ultimate values in order of their importance to you from 1 to 10, with 1 being the most valued and 10 the least. If you're not sure about some of them, don't worry. We're not looking for something too detailed, just a general picture of the kinds of values that matter most to you.

If you find yourself stuck trying to figure out which values are more important to you, here are a couple of tricks. First, your values are often reflected in your attitudes or interests. As you consider each of the ten ultimate values, pay attention to the positive feelings you have associated with them. You might naturally feel a gravity toward science and an aversion toward security. Maybe aesthetics is what captures your interest.

Another way to help you determine your values hierarchy is to consider how you've spent your time over the past week, month, or year. What activities have dominated your schedule, and what values do they reflect? Do you spend a lot of time working late at the office? Could that be a reflection of the fact that you value commerce and want to make sure your company is profitable? Alternatively, it could be a reflection of the fact that you want to be recognized by your boss or your peers as someone who puts in the extra time it takes to succeed.

As you make your own list, are you surprised by the results? Does your values hierarchy line up with how you think of yourself? If you're courageous enough, right now is a great time to share your values hierarchy with the support network you identified in the introduction. Ask them to let you know if they agree with your assessment of your values or if they might have a different perspective.

MIND THE GAPS

It is common to encounter discrepancies between your values hierarchy and how others see you. These discrepancies are natural, and provide you with an opportunity to push deeper. Why, for example, might you have ranked "altruism" higher on your list than your network did?

Often, the difference between what you think you value and what others see as your values is the result of character issues. Character, remember, is a reflection of your moral strength—your ability to act in ways that might be unpopular or run counter to your own self-interest or ego. If there are some gaps in your character, it can often distort how your values are showing up in your life.

As you continue to explore your character and values, please be patient with yourself. None of us are perfect, and the whole point of the Intelligent Leadership process is to identify the ways we can improve ourselves and make a bigger impact in the world. If you were to breeze through this exercise with little to no difficulty, I'd guess that you were either a perfect human being or not being diligent enough. I'll let you determine which one is more likely.

As we progress through *The Intelligent Leader*, we'll be exploring how each of the seven dimensions are rooted in and influenced by your character and values. They are the foundation of who we are, and if we want to develop into a powerful expression of great leadership, getting deeply familiar with our character and values is essential.

WHO DO YOU THINK YOU ARE?

The final components of our inner core are our self-concept and beliefs. These are how our deeper character and values are translated into our outer core behaviors and capabilities. Unlike your character and your values, which can often be mostly unconscious, your self-concept and beliefs are more likely to be elements of yourself you're more aware of.

Self-concept is, quite simply, how you think of yourself. Do you consider yourself to be a successful person or a failure? A leader or a follower? An extrovert or an introvert? Your self-concept will, to a significant degree, shape the kind of person, and leader, that the world experiences. And many areas in which you are weak in terms of leadership can often be traced back to some kind of issue with your self-concept.

For example, if you tend to think of yourself as a victim of circumstance, then you might consistently find yourself unable to navigate challenging situations. You'll always feel powerless to rise up and overcome the burdens you encounter. But if you see yourself as a problem solver, you will be more likely to take responsibility for yourself and those around you, regardless of your situation.

The best leaders tend to have a very positive self-concept. This can be the result of a naturally positive outlook on life, which might come from your family or cultural upbringing, but it can also be the result of continued reinforcement of that positive image based on past successes. If you have continuously overcome obstacles in your life, you're likely to have more confidence in your ability to navigate challenges in the future. You've proven it to yourself and built a stronger self-concept in the process.

This is good news. It means that even if you find that your self-concept isn't as positive as you'd like it to be, you can change it. Self-concept, much like the other elements of your inner core, is quite malleable. Through self-examination and practice, you can literally overhaul your self-concept for the better.

As we move through the seven dimensions of Intelligent Leadership, I'll be providing you with exercises that will help you to build a stronger and more positive self-concept. Each dimension will shine new light on your existing self-concept and an opportunity to grow and expand it.

BELIEVE IT OR NOT . . .

Beliefs are closely tied to your self-concept. When you hear the word "belief," it is often used to describe ideas or notions you have based more on faith or intuition than on evidence or fact. This might be a belief in some kind of higher power or a belief in the inherent goodness of people.

When I talk about beliefs, however, I mean something slightly different. The beliefs that I'm looking for are the principles that we know to be true through repeated experience. For instance, we might believe that human beings are inherently good, because we've repeatedly experienced acts of goodness and kindness by others in our lives. This deeply held belief, then, shapes how we act in the world. It creates a sense of optimism and unlimited possibility in how we assess and interact with others, because we believe that down deep there is goodness inside of everyone.

Another example I frequently encounter in leaders is an unconscious belief that people aren't capable of real change. While they might never admit it, or even know it's part of their worldview, they carry a conviction that people are who they are and can't really change in significant ways. This could come from years of accepting the way things are or it could come from earlier childhood experiences. In any case, by carrying this belief, they are sabotaging their own efforts to change, because deep down they don't think it's actually possible.

Beliefs, in this context, have a powerful effect on the type of person we are and the kind of potential we have as leaders. One of the goals of Intelligent Leadership is to unpack the beliefs you have, determine which of them are holding you back, and then start to build new belief systems that will support your growth as a leader and a human being.

Measuring Your Inner Core with the Mattone Leadership Enneagram Inventory (MLEI)

In my 2013 book, *Intelligent Leadership*, I explored in great depth the Mattone Leadership Enneagram Inventory (MLEI), a tool that I created in 1996 to help leaders and aspiring leaders assess their own strengths and developmental needs. The MLEI, which is now based on data from over 10,000 global leaders, draws upon an ancient model (some trace its origins to Babylon in 2500 BCE) for understanding the unique maturities and perspectives that each of us possess. The word enneagram itself comes from the Greek words *ennea*, meaning "nine" and *gram*, meaning "something written or drawn."

Each of the nine points on the enneagram corresponds to a distinct way of thinking, feeling, and behavioral tendencies (Figure 1.2). Thus, people at different points on the enneagram

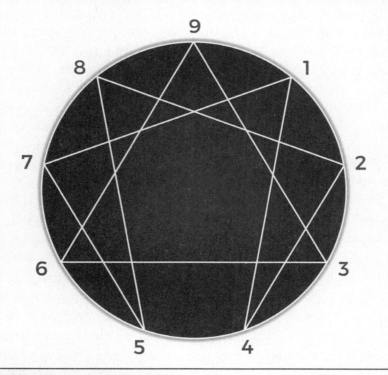

FIGURE 1.2   The enneagram.

view the world and interact with it differently. When you engage with the enneagram, through a series of questions, you're able to identify which areas you're stronger in and those where you need development. It's literally a window into the specific makeup of your inner core.

The enneagram works. That's why it continues to be used after thousands of years. With the MLEI, I've applied the enneagram model directly to the realm of leadership. Many other approaches focus primarily on changing behaviors. But without understanding why you act the way you do, you usually fall back to your original behavioral patterns after a short time. The MLEI is developed to provide a deep foundation of self-understanding that will help to make any of the development work you're doing stick.

We won't spend a lot of time talking about the MLEI in this book, but if you're interested in gaining a greater understanding of your own strengths and weaknesses, I highly recommend that you go through the process yourself. It's free to you, the reader, at this link: Johnmattone.com/booktools.

THE BRIDGE TO THE OUTER CORE

At this point you are hopefully beginning to get a sense of just what your inner core is and why it's so important to developing your leadership capacity. But you might also be wondering just exactly *how* all this exploration of your inner core is supposed to help you make a real impact on yourself, your career, and the world.

That's a natural question. Most people I work with are seeking leadership development, not character improvement or self-knowledge. They are looking to have a bigger impact in their careers. They want to improve their skills and capabilities so that they can perform at a higher level and help their teams, companies, and organizations to do the same. What they really want to improve is their outer core, which I define simply as the behaviors, skills, and competencies they bring to the world and, as a result, the impact they have on those around them.

Your outer core represents the kinds of qualities that show up on performance reviews and 360-degree surveys, and the kinds of qualities that people either praise or criticize you for. They include things like your ability to make decisions or think strategically and critically. They include your ability to communicate and listen effectively and your overall emotional intelligence. One of the most important elements of your outer core has to do with your ability to lead a team and to cultivate talent within your organization.

In my experience, if you want to improve your outer core in a significant way, you've got to start with your inner core values, character, and beliefs. To me, this is a non-negotiable. Values and beliefs, sitting on the foundation of your character, are what ultimately drive your actions and are the key to unlocking and unleashing your full potential. The old cliché is true: "actions speak louder than words." If you want to get a sense of who someone is (their character) and what they value, all you need to do is take a look at their actions.

For example, you may say that you're someone who values innovation and cutting-edge thinking, but you might also experience a kind of fear or rigidity when encountering new ideas, especially when those new ideas come from someone other than you. This might reveal that you actually value security, tradition, and power more than you thought.

These are the kind of paradoxes and contradictions we're looking for. We want to find the ways in which your behavior is not lining up with your values, character, self-concept, and beliefs. This can be difficult, and even embarrassing at first. But these quirks are actually really positive signs. They are opportunities for growth and greater alignment.

This is why it is so profoundly important to get to know your inner core when you're trying to make real and lasting change in your capacities, skills, and behavior. Your outer core is the impact you make in the world. And you'll never be able to change that impact unless you start to understand the ways in which your outer core is driven by your inner core.

With Intelligent Leadership, our outer core competencies and behavior are not where we start. They are the result of the work we do at deeper levels. They are also "leading indicators" of how we are doing and where we may need to look more closely. They are ultimately what we are trying to evolve, but they are literally the tips of the iceberg sitting atop an extraordinary amount of depth below the surface.

PUTTING IT ALL TOGETHER: THE SPECTRUM
OF INTELLIGENT LEADERSHIP

When my latest grandchild was born, my wife and I purchased a mobile to hang next to the window in his nursery, just above the crib. The mobile was crafted by a local artist and includes a menagerie of polished myrtle wood pieces dangling from fishing line surrounding a globe-shaped crystal hanging in the center of the arrangement. To our grandson's delight, the morning light from the window shines through the crystal globe and casts rainbow-colored light patterns on all the walls and ceiling of the nursery. It's a magical sight to behold, and likely one you've experienced in one way or another in your own life.

The interplay of light and the crystal is a perfect metaphor for the dynamic between the inner and outer core. And it's a metaphor that I will use throughout the book along with the model we've been exploring throughout this chapter. Our inner core, which consists of our character, our deep-seated values, our self-concept, and our beliefs, is the crystal. The outer core, which is what the world sees—our personality, our skills and competencies—is the pattern of colors projected onto everything around us.

At heart of this dynamic are the seven dimensions of Intelligent Leadership. They permeate the crystal and influence the shape and vibrancy of the color patterns cast on the walls around us. The seven dimensions, which we will spend the remainder of the book exploring are:

1. Thinking Differently, Thinking Big
2. The Vulnerability Decision
3. Having a Mindset of Entitlement versus a Mindset of Duty
4. Leveraging Your Gifts and Addressing Your Gaps
5. Having the Courage to Execute with Pride, Passion, and Precision
6. Staying Present and Being Vigilant
7. Course Correction

Think of each of the seven dimensions as being equal parts inner and outer core—a kind of connective tissue that binds them together. These are the unique qualities that collectively make up the true essence of great leadership. These seven dimensions are the gateway that simultaneously gives us access to better understanding our inner core and the amplifiers that help our light to shine more beautifully, vibrantly, and powerfully through our actions.

Figure 1.3 shows the seven dimensions that make up Intelligent Leadership. As you can see, each dimension is rooted in the inner core and reflected in the outer core. Each dimension, by itself, represents a goal to achieve, master, and optimize as a foundation to positively transforming yourself as a leader and human being. Interestingly, the seven dimensions also represent a pathway you can take to ensure a positive transformation that sticks. In many ways, the seven dimensions represent the "mindset of change" you must possess in order to become a great leader.

Over the next seven chapters, we will explore each of the seven dimensions. Each chapter will show you exactly what each dimension looks like and how you can apply it to develop your own leadership mindset. As we explore each dimension, we'll discover how they are rooted in our inner core and how they express themselves in our increased capacity for demonstrating great leadership. By developing each of these dimensions in yourself, you will not only gain a deeper, richer understanding of what may or may not be

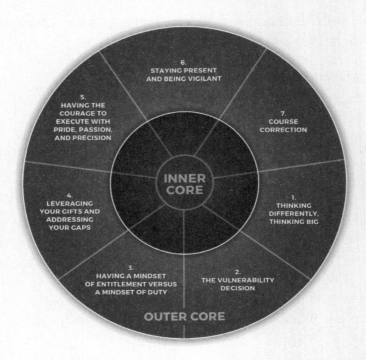

FIGURE 1.3   The seven dimensions of Intelligent Leadership.

working to your benefit in your inner core, you'll also expand your ability to translate what you discover into actionable behaviors that will strengthen your outer core. Ultimately, it is this work alone—and how diligent you are in doing it—that will shape, define, and determine your success as a person and leader.

FAKE IT 'TIL YOU MAKE IT

When I played baseball as a kid, one of my favorite coaches was fond of using the phrase "fake it 'til you make it" whenever introducing a new skill to the team. Essentially, that means that you pretend as if you can do something until you're actually able to do it. Even before you have mastered a new skill, you are putting yourself in the *mindset* of someone who possesses it, which accelerates the process.

Over the years, I've come to appreciate the wisdom of this approach to development and found it to be useful for more than just learning to hit a curveball.

So in each chapter of the book, I'll be providing you with what I call "igniting behaviors" that you can put into practice in order to start to truly master the mindset of each Intelligent Leadership dimension.

These behaviors will help you to actively shift your inner core by acting in ways, sometimes small and sometimes big, that reflect the mindset of great leadership you're trying to achieve. This process can be uncomfortable at first, because you're doing things that don't feel natural. But over time, as you continue to act in new and positive ways, you'll start to find that you are, without thinking, being driven by an Intelligent Leadership mindset, and the results in your performance and impact on those around you will begin to flow naturally.

CHAPTER 2

Thinking Differently, Thinking Big

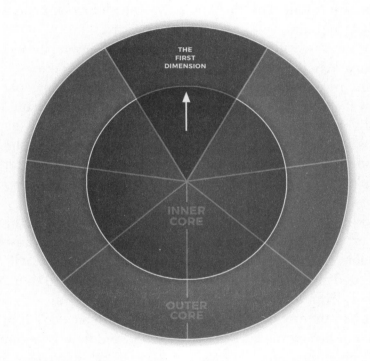

When you read the title of this chapter, you might think of Steve Jobs and Apple computer's classic 1997 advertising campaign. If you aren't old enough to remember the ad, which many consider the greatest marketing campaign of all time, google it. The TV commercial at the center of the campaign, which marked Jobs's return to Apple after a fifteen-year absence, features a series of clips of history's great minds—Einstein, Dylan, Earhart, King Jr, Lennon, Ali—while a voice reads: "Because the people who are crazy enough to think they can change the world, are the ones who do." As the screen goes to black, the words "Think Different" along with the Apple Macintosh logo appear, accompanied by silence.

It's a powerful message, even today. At the time, it was revolutionary. When Jobs unveiled the campaign during one of his now iconic "reveal" speeches, it drew a standing ovation. People didn't know it at the time, but the "Think Different" tagline would eventually become synonymous with the Apple brand, and shape the ethos of a company that brought us some of the most revolutionary technologies in history. And "thinking differently" has, for many people, become an essential quality of twenty-first-century leadership—for others, a way of life.

So I have to give Jobs and the late '90s Apple marketing team at least some credit for inspiring the first dimension of Intelligent Leadership. But I didn't just cherry-pick it from them, willy-nilly. I learned about the power of thinking differently and thinking big directly from Jobs himself.

I had the privilege of working with Steve as a coach in 2010. This was during the later years of his life, and he was beginning to think about his legacy. He wanted me to help him go deep into his own inner core so he could make sure to have the biggest impact on the world—his family, friends, company, and beyond—before he passed on.

I can honestly say that even though Jobs had hired *me* to be his leadership coach, I learned more from him than he learned from me. This may not seem that surprising, given that Jobs is considered to be one of the brightest and most influential minds of his generation. But what made the deepest impression on me wasn't necessarily his brilliance; it was the profound sense of purpose that he felt driving his career. There was one exchange in particular that I will never forget—one that ultimately shaped my own approach to leadership development.

"Mattone," he said (he never used my first name during our sessions), "I want to tell you something that I've shared with very few people before." He had my attention. He continued, "You remember the Think Different campaign, right?"

"Of course," I said.

"Well, that initiative was definitely centered around relaunching the Apple brand and selling our products, but when I took the stage that day to give my speech, I was in many respects speaking symbolically."

That struck me and I asked him, "What do you mean by 'symbolically'?" His answer gave me chills. It went something like this:

"I knew this was my one opportunity to share, not only with my people at Apple, but with the entire world, everything I had learned during my fifteen years away from the company. During that time, I did a lot of soul searching and grew tremendously, both as a leader and a person. What I learned became one of the key tenets that Apple was built on: If you want to get different results in your personal life or in your businesses—if that is the vision that you embrace—then you have to have the courage to step outside of your comfort zone and disrupt yourself. You have to be willing to think as big as possible about yourself and what you have to contribute to the world."

For Jobs, "Think Different" was more like a spiritual epiphany than it was a marketing slogan. The marketing campaign—he revealed to me—was just an excuse to share that epiphany with the world. And it worked. A whole generation of people has been inspired, not just by the awesomeness of Apple's products (sorry, if you're an Android or PC person), but also by the philosophy that Steve laid out that day.

Thinking differently and thinking big has become a cornerstone of my own work, because I've found—over and over again—that if you want to become a truly great leader, it all starts with your mindset. If you really want to become something more, to change, to become something different, it's inevitable that you're also going to have to change the way you think. You're going to have to leap into a bigger view of yourself and the world and, in the process, you might have to leave behind some of your older, more narrow ways of thinking. You've got to be willing to think differently than you have before, bigger than you have before.

This insight is the primary step on the journey of Intelligent Leadership. That's why I've made this the first dimension of Intelligent Leadership. It's a non-negotiable tenet of becoming a truly great leader.

In this chapter, we're going to unpack what thinking differently and thinking big actually looks like, why it's so crucial to strong leadership, and how you can start to embrace this mindset in your own life.

BEING A TRENDSETTER

At the beginning of the book we defined leadership simply as "an example for others to follow." One of the qualities that attract people to great leaders is their ability to think outside the box—to innovate new approaches to common issues that change the course of any initiative, whether it's a project, a business, or an entire country. Being willing to question the "status quo" within whatever context you're operating can help set the tone for your team. And if you're striving to think differently yourself, you'll encourage the same in those around you. You'll create a culture of innovation and evolution.

Steve Jobs is, of course, a perfect example of this quality. He had an uncanny ability to think about technology through the eyes of the user while so many of his competitors were ignoring—or not placing enough value on—this essential component of the human-technology interface. His dedication to empowering individuals through technology changed the game forever, bringing us everything from the personal computer, to the iPod, to the smartphone. He wasn't afraid to think differently, and he changed the world.

Thanks in part to Jobs, "thinking differently" has become pretty sexy in our world today. Who wouldn't want to be an innovator or revolutionary thinker? But a big part of thinking differently is having the courage and strength of character to stand behind your ideas when they aren't popular. Thinking differently, by definition, will place you directly at odds with the status quo. You may have heard the story of the Oakland As in the early part of this century, as portrayed in the movie *Moneyball* starring Brad Pitt. The legendary general manager Billy Beane changed the game of baseball forever by his outside-the-box thinking. The Oakland As were on the brink of irrelevance in 2002, with little budget and an even worse roster. Beane partnered with a little-known Yale economics grad named Peter Brand (portrayed by Jonah Hill in the film), who had a radical approach to recruiting new talent based on complex math and statistics. Unsurprisingly, Beane faced outrageous resistance to his broad-scale implementation of Brand's approach—from his coach and players, from his fellow GMs, from the sports media, and even the fans. But Beane stuck to his instincts and didn't compromise, and by the end of the season he took his likely bottom-dwelling team into the playoffs. His willingness to think differently, and stand behind that thinking, eventually changed the entire culture of professional baseball.

And yet, the "thinking differently" mindset isn't as common among top business leaders as you might think. Avra Lyraki is an executive coaching colleague of mine from Greece who has spent most of her career in human resource development and corporate communications across several different industries. She's found that the whole notion of thinking differently terrifies most of the CEOs she works with. While they are powerful individuals with a lot of extraordinary leadership qualities, they tend to be more conservative in their thinking.

This makes sense. When you're in a position of authority, there's a tremendous amount of pressure and responsibility on your shoulders. You are beholden to your investors, your board, your employees, your customers, your clients. You don't want to make mistakes, because there's so much riding on your decisions. So CEOs tend to be very risk averse. As long as things are running smoothly, profits are trending in the right direction, and there are no big problems, the most logical path often seems to be keeping things stable and consistent.

There is, of course, a lot of value to this more conservative mentality. As a leader, you can't be disrupting and challenging the status quo *all* the time. You've got to create some stability for your team. It's also important to build on the time-tested elements of your strategy and systems that are really working. But if you don't also include a dose of disruption from time to time, and keep yourself open to new ideas, opportunities, and ways of doing business, you're bound to get stale and fall behind.

HOLDING A MASSIVE VISION

In his address to United States Congress on May 25, 1961, President John F. Kennedy uttered a bold claim: by the end of the decade, the United States would put a man on the moon. It was a radical statement, and met with a lot of skepticism. At the time, the U.S. space program was not evolving at a pace nearly fast enough to achieve such a massive goal, lagging significantly behind its Cold War rival, the U.S.S.R., and few people thought it could be done. But Kennedy, no doubt supported by his advisors, saw a different possibility for Project Apollo. By making such a public declaration on that day, he put a figurative stake in the ground that would mobilize the political, economic, and financial resources necessary to make such a seemingly impossible goal achievable. Eight years later, just before the decade ended, Kennedy's vision was made reality as Neil Armstrong took those first lunar steps, with the whole world watching.

Kennedy, like so many great leaders, understood the power of holding a big vision in order to bring something new into existence. This is one of the key dimensions of intelligent leadership: if you want to lead, you need to have the ability to inspire people to think about themselves, their lives, and their work, in a bigger context. You have to cultivate, at least to some degree, a capacity to create an overarching purpose to which others can orient themselves.

This requires a lot of personal courage. Thinking big moves people out of their comfort zones, which can be scary. Most people, whether they'll admit it or not, aren't that interested in "thinking big." They're satisfied with the status quo, of achieving a basic amount of security, and simply living their lives rather than shooting for a more significant outcome. Even the idea of "thinking big" can make the hair stand up on the back of their necks. Give it a try: imagine a big vision for yourself—becoming wildly successful, pursuing a dream you've always had but never gone for, stepping up to a new level of leadership in some area of your life. I'd bet that there's at least some small part of you that's afraid of the vision you're holding—a part of yourself that wants absolutely nothing to do with the success or change that you're conjuring.

If you're finding any personal resistance to thinking big, it's okay. That's a natural response. The status quo isn't just something "out there" in society or an organization; it's also something inside all of us. This is a useful inner voice in many circumstances. It's a healthy fear of disruption and the unknown that keeps us grounded. It's the well-hewn path of comfort and stability that makes many things in our world possible.

But if you want to be a leader, you need to learn to see this fear of big thinking for what it is, and occasionally take action in spite of it. You've got to have the courage to throw down your own "man on the moon" declaration, whether it be for yourself or for something bigger, and then muster the resources to make it a reality.

The Long Game

An important subset of thinking big is the capacity to hold a long-term view when dealing with the day-to-day workings of any organization or campaign. This is crucial to implementing your own "Project Apollo" and the inevitable setbacks, scrutiny, and resistance to change that such an initiative will face. Amazon CEO Jeff Bezos has a powerful perspective on long-term thinking, which he shared in a 2011 *U.S. News & World Report* interview with David LaGesse:

> My own view is that every company needs a long-term view. If you're going to take a long-term orientation, you have to be willing to stay "heads down" and ignore a wide array of critics, even well-meaning critics. If you don't have a willingness to be misunderstood for a long period of time, then you can't have a long-term orientation. Because we have done it many times and have come out the other side, we have enough internal stories that we can tell ourselves. While we're crossing the desert, we may be thirsty, but we sincerely believe there's an oasis on the other side.

HOW BIG DO YOU THINK?

At this point, I hope you're starting to reflect on just how much you embody the qualities of thinking differently and thinking big. In my experience, this kind of reflection can go in a couple different directions. You might already consider yourself to be the kind of leader who isn't afraid of shaking things up by thinking outside the box or creating a big vision for your team; you might see a lot of yourself in the examples I've given so far. On the other hand, you might be feeling somewhat intimidated by all of it, and feeling that it just doesn't fit who you are. Or you might be feeling some mixture of both.

No matter the case, if you want to cultivate this dimension of leadership in yourself, or amplify the qualities you already embody, it's important to do some reflection.

Below are a series of qualities and behaviors that are often associated with thinking differently and thinking big. These are "leading indicators" of how much you embody this dimension of leadership, and are meant to help you measure yourself so you can determine what areas need improvement. They are also behaviors that you can put into practice right away to help expand the way you think.

As you read them, I encourage you to reflect upon how much you do or don't consistently exhibit these behaviors. Once you've gone through them yourself, reach out to your support network and ask them if they agree with your assessment.

Setting Aside Time Just to Think

One of the keys to expanding your ability to think is to set aside the time to do just that: think. I'm talking about time that is free from competing stimuli, distraction, and interruptions, in which you can let your mind roam freely and focus on things beyond the day-to-day demands of your life.

During this time, you can focus on the future—and envision a new and more compelling future than you have now. In your mind's eye, concretely isolate a new compelling goal, pursuit, and vision.

Most people never take the opportunity to think about the future in new ways because they are mired in the demands of the present or the regrets of the past. But one of the keys to being a big thinker, is setting aside time to consistently practice big thinking, whether it's daily, weekly, or monthly. There are a lot of ways to do this—taking walks, meditation, or just sitting quietly in your office or home. You can find whatever works best for you. My best thinking happens on long flights. I never watch movies or listen to music. I make a point to completely "unplug," which entirely unclutters my mind so I can think in a limitless way.

Remaining Open to All Potential Ideas and Opportunities

One of the most common limiting factors to big thinking is the tendency that many people have to dismiss potential opportunities prematurely. That's why it's so important to cultivate a habit of saying "yes" before "no" when it comes to new ideas. This can apply to ideas that come both from others and from yourself.

In 2016, I received a call from a human resources consulting firm based in Gaborone, Botswana. They wanted to invite me for three days to teach their partners everything I knew about executive coaching. I was reluctant to go because I was afraid they wouldn't be able to pay me. Years earlier, I had taken another gig in Botswana and been cheated out of half of my fees, so I had a lot of reservations. But I also had an intuition that this was important for me to do. I took a risk and accepted the job.

At the time, my coaching process and philosophy had never been pulled together into one place. There was no comprehensive "Intelligent Leadership" manual or book, and I knew that I would need one in order to effectively train the partners of this HR consulting firm. So I put in the work to bring it all together and ended up with a 600-page manual. It was by no means perfect, but the Botswana team found it very useful. This gave me an idea. If I could further improve my coach education materials, I could create a whole process for training and certifying coaches to become more effective. And so I did.

This initial experience eventually led to the development of my Intelligent Leadership Executive Coaching Certification program, which has become the most successful element of my business and my brand. I've personally coached and certified over 400 coaches since March 2017 from 47 different countries, and we're just getting started.

I tell this story not to try and impress you, but to impress upon you how important it is to remain open. Had I simply written off the Botswana gig as a dead end, I never would have had the impetus to start my coach training program. Because I was open to possibilities that I couldn't see, I encountered a significant opportunity that changed the course of my career.

Zeroing in on What Is Real and Actionable

As you practice the art of thinking differently and thinking big, it's important, at least initially, to let your mind roam limitlessly. But eventually, you will want to move toward ideas and perspectives that can be put into action in the real world. Any idea, no matter how revolutionary, is only as good as it is actionable. And if you don't hold yourself to this standard, your "big thinking" won't actually go anywhere and you'll get cynical.

So as you hone in on new ideas and prospective courses of action, make sure to break them up into smaller pieces until each one feels doable. As you encounter new problems, think through several realistic solutions. Contrary to how it appears on the surface, applying rigor to your big ideas won't limit you. It will provide solid ground upon which to bring new realities into being.

Bouncing Your Ideas Off Others

The old adage "two heads are better than one" is especially true when it comes to big thinking. In my experience, the best ideas are often generated through the course of conversation with others. There's a mysterious kind of alchemy that happens when you bounce your ideas around with one or more people. They bring different perspectives that, when mixed with your own, can create new angles and possibilities that you wouldn't have generated on your own.

So when you're trying to think differently and think big, it's invaluable to share your ideas with your most trusted stakeholders, at least initially. This, of course, comes with challenges. You need to have the maturity to handle constructive feedback effectively. You need to be able to hold your ego in check to some degree so that you can allow your ideas to become more than you had originally conceived.

BEGINNING WITH THE END IN MIND

Now that you've had a chance to reflect on your own capacity to think differently and think big, you might be wondering what you can do to cultivate these capacities in yourself. Even if you consider yourself to be already strong in this dimension—an out-of-the-box thinker and visionary type—and others perceive you this way, there's always room to amplify these qualities in order to have an even more significant impact. The question is, how?

The biggest mistake that people make when trying to apply this dimension of Intelligent Leadership is thinking that they need to *will* their way into some new form of behavior. Their minds immediately go to strategizing ways that they can think outside the box in their personal or work life, or they sit down and try to conjure the biggest vision for their life or company possible.

These are, of course, natural responses. They're also useful, but only to a limited degree. Like so many dimensions of Intelligent Leadership, thinking differently and thinking big require that you work at a deeper level than your outer core behaviors and dive into your inner core. This is what Steve Jobs did during the fifteen years of soul-searching that he did en route to his revolutionary return to Apple. And the conduit to your inner core is getting in touch with what I call your "core purpose."

What do I mean by "core purpose"? When it comes to Intelligent Leadership, understanding your core purpose is the ultimate form of big thinking. It starts with asking yourself the really big questions:

- Why am I here?
- What was I put on this earth to do?
- What is the unique gift that I offer to the world?

Grappling with your core purpose is meant to throw your life and personal pursuits into the biggest and brightest possible light. From here, you can see your tremendous potential—and also the many ways in which you may be unconsciously holding that potential back.

Billions and Billions

When I'm looking for a bigger perspective on my place in the universe, I like to take a page out of the playbook of the late astronomer Carl Sagan. Sagan had a penchant for describing the indescribable vastness of the cosmos in a way that made it immediately relevant to our lives, and his catchphrase "billions and billions," used to describe the infinite number of stars in the universe, inspired a generation to look upward with a new sense of awe and wonder.

One of my favorite tricks for getting in touch with a deeper sense of purpose is to spend some time looking up at the night sky and contemplating the fact that we are all floating on a tiny little planet in the midst of an incomprehensibly large universe. It makes this moment in time and space seem precious, and it adds a new level of focus, clarity, and significance to how I view my short time here.

It may sound hokey, but this kind of contemplation works. You may have a different trick for expanding your perspective, or a time-tested practice that you use to connect to a larger view on your experience. It doesn't really matter what you do, as long as you're making an effort to get outside of yourself and see your life in the biggest possible context.

This kind of inquiry can be challenging at first, because most of us aren't used to thinking about ourselves, or our lives, in a context this big. Many of us avoid asking these questions because we're afraid of what we'll find out. I've worked with many successful executives in their sixties who have never before asked themselves these questions. They've either never considered doing so, or on some level have been avoiding the questions for fear of where the answers might lead them.

This is the paradox of change. On one level, we all desire to become more, reach our potential, and have a massive impact on the world. But on another level, we are deeply afraid of the kind of havoc that this kind of change will wreak in our lives. Many of us are more addicted to the status quo than we realize, or care to admit, and are often quite comfortable with living a life that is merely adequate.

The truth is that we need more leaders who are willing to ask these big questions. We owe it to ourselves, but more importantly, we owe it to the people relying on us—our families, our teams, our organizations. If you really want to be someone who makes a truly positive impact on the world around you, then you need to go this deep. The reward is well worth it. The same executive clients who had never before done this kind of inquiry have experienced profound results from daring to think of their lives in this big context. They have discovered gifts and strengths in themselves that have been hidden to them their entire lives.

Can you see how this inquiry will allow you to embody the spirit of Jobs's "Think Different" campaign? To create your own personal Apollo project? Those people who are deeply connected to who they are and why they're here on this earth exude a kind of clarity that can cut through any kind of resistance—internal or external. This is the key to being a truly independent thinker and leader. "Purpose-driven" leaders have an orientation point that all their actions are moving toward, and a solid inner foundation that allows them to express their unique perspectives and gifts, regardless of the status quo.

So, I ask you, do you know what your purpose is? Do you know what you were put on this earth to do?

DON'T LET YOUR BIG THINKING GIVE YOU A BIG HEAD

I believe that there's a healthy and unhealthy expression of every human quality, including the dimensions of IL. Each dimension of IL should be balanced with all the others so that one quality isn't exaggerated over the others. It's like the old saying "everything in moderation." As we progress through the chapters ahead, we will explore the ways in which the various dimensions of IL interact with one another to create a powerful expression of leadership. And we will also highlight the potential pitfalls that can be found in each dimension when not properly balanced.

Having too much of thinking differently and thinking big, for example, can lead to arrogance and the inability to build strong relationships. Steve Jobs himself embodied both the good and the bad of big thinking. His unwillingness to compromise at times made him difficult to work with. Jobs's intense commitment to always thinking different often created a sense of superiority and kept him on the outside of the many relationships he held in his career. It has been reported by many that he drove people too hard, often in pursuit of big thinking, which contributed to his being fired by Apple in 1985. If you are too focused on your big vision, and overlooking the important details and relationships that it takes to make that vision a reality, then you can find yourself in a similar position to Jobs.

So as you engage with this dimension of IL, make sure to keep your ego in check. Pay attention to how your big thinking is affecting others, and be aware of your underlying motives. One of the telltale signs that thinking big is giving you a big head is that you start to be more interested in appearing to be the one with the new ideas than you are in the ideas themselves. You may have trouble with big, new ideas that aren't coming from you, and feel competitive with others who are exercising this dimension of IL.

Don't worry—this tendency is only natural, and it's easy to course correct if you find your ego getting in the way. You simply need to stay aware, and then recalibrate if you see any negative consequences starting to emerge. Do whatever you need to do to keep yourself humble. Return to your core purpose statement and ask yourself if your current behavior is in line with that big vision. The other dimensions of IL can also help you to stay humble, particularly the next two: The Vulnerability Decision and Having a Mindset of Duty. When exercised in combination, as we'll explore later, these three dimensions of IL create a powerful balance of confidence, strength, and humility that will supercharge your leadership capacities.

EXERCISE: DEVELOPING YOUR CORE PURPOSE STATEMENT

To help you get connected to your own deeper purpose, I'd like to introduce an exercise I do with all my clients at the very beginning of our work together: creating a "core purpose statement" (CPS). This is a simple description of the biggest and most fundamental vision you can articulate for yourself. Your CPS should capture the essence of the person you want to become, what qualities you want to develop, what you want to accomplish, and what contributions you want to make. Your CPS is meant to become your personal constitution, the basis for navigating the many decisions—both simple and profound—that you encounter throughout your life.

Creating a CPS is actually quite common among leaders. Here are some great examples from successful CEOs:

- **Denise Morrison, CEO of Campbell Soup Company**: *To serve as a leader, live a balanced life, and apply ethical principles to make a significant difference.*
- **Joel Manby, CEO of Herschend Family Entertainment**: *I define personal success as being consistent to my own personal mission statement: to love God and love others.*
- **Oprah Winfrey, founder of OWN, the Oprah Winfrey Network:** *To be a teacher. And to be known for inspiring my students to be more than they thought they could be.*
- **Sir Richard Branson, founder of the Virgin Group:** *To have fun in [my] journey through life and learn from [my] mistakes.*
- **Amanda Steinberg, founder of DailyWorth.com:** *To use my gifts of intelligence, charisma, and serial optimism to cultivate the self-worth and net-worth of women around the world.*

While the examples above are all one sentence long, an effective CPS may consist of a few words or several pages. It can be written in poetry, prose, music, or art. To give you a sense of a different kind of CPS, here's one that I did for myself:

I want to develop self-knowledge, self-love, and self-allowing. I want to use my healing talents to keep hope alive and express my vision courageously in word and action. In my family, I want to build healthy, loving relationships in which we let each other become our best selves. At work, I want to establish a fault-free, self-perpetuating, learning environment. In the world, I want to nurture the development of all life forms, in harmony with the laws of nature. To act in a manner that brings out the best in me and those important to me, especially when it might be most justifiable to act otherwise.

Now that you've seen some examples of what a CPS looks like, it's time to make one of your own. To guide you through the process, I've put together a series of questions that will help you to hone in on your CPS. Do your best to answer these questions as fully as you can prior to making your first draft.

As you go through the exercise, it's important that you don't become overwhelmed or feel the need to make it perfect. Writing an empowering CPS is not a "to do" to be checked off. It is a living document. You must ponder it, memorize it, review it, update it, and write it into your heart and mind.

To help you get started, ask yourself the following questions:

- What would I really like to be and do in my life?
- What are my greatest strengths?
- How do I want to be remembered?
- Who is the one person who has made the greatest positive impact in my life?
- What have been my happiest moments in life?
- If I had unlimited time and resources, what would I do?
- If I were to do one thing in my *professional* life that would have the most positive impact, what would it be?
- If I were to do one thing in my *personal* life that would have the most positive impact, what would it be?

- What are the three or four most important things to me?
- How can I best contribute to the world?

Now, project yourself forward. Visualize the end of life. You are surrounded by your loved ones, friends, and the colleagues you have touched along your life's journey. One by one they lean over to whisper their final words to you.

- What would each person whisper to you?
- What difference have you made in their life?
- What qualities or characteristics will you be remembered for?
- What outstanding contribution of yours would they mention?

Now that you've gone through the preparatory questions, you're now ready to write a draft of your core purpose statement. Again, your CPS can be anywhere from a sentence to a page long, and take any form that will have the most value for you. Write a draft and then let it sit for some time. Return to it in a couple of days or a week and look at it with fresh eyes. Adjust as necessary and keep returning to it as often as you need.

This exercise is one of the most important things you can do to connect to your inner core, which is the source of your leadership potential—and human potential. If you take it seriously, you will find that, in the process, you begin to naturally embody the first dimension of Intelligent Leadership, and exhibit the "Think Different" mentality that has driven so many great leaders throughout history. Try it. I guarantee you'll be happy with the results.

CHAPTER 3

The Vulnerability Decision

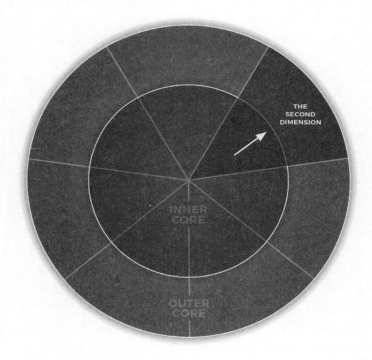

When I was a kid, John Wayne was one of the biggest movie stars in the land. "The Duke," as he was called, played the heroic lead in countless Westerns and war movies from the late 1930s through the 1960s, and cemented himself in the pantheon of American icons as the ultimate strongman. His influence was so broad that his name has, in many ways, become shorthand for being a "man's man," meaning someone who uses toughness and intimidation to get what he wants in the world, keeping thoughts and feelings to himself, and never showing weakness.

In his 2014 biography, *John Wayne: The Life and Legend*, Scott Eyman recounts a story that perfectly illuminates the role that Wayne played (and in some respects, continues to play) in society. At a party in 1957, it's reported that Wayne confronted his fellow actor Kirk Douglas, a fellow "tough guy" famous for movies like *Spartacus*. Wayne was upset about Douglas's decision to play the role of Vincent van Gogh—an artist who represented a more sensitive side of masculinity—in the film *Lust for Life*. He reportedly said, "Christ, Kirk, how can you play a part like that? There's so goddamn few of us left. We got to play strong, tough characters." Strength and toughness were, for the Duke, part of the identity he spent his life building, maintaining, and ultimately inspiring in millions of his fans.

The "John Wayne" mentality is woven so deeply into the fabric of American culture that generations of people—men and women—who have never even seen one of his movies are influenced by his tough-guy approach to life. And there may be no arena in society where this influence is more pronounced than in leadership—especially corporate leadership. Indeed, most of the CEOs I work with subscribe to the John Wayne school of leadership—no nonsense, toughness at all costs, never showing weakness or vulnerability. Even many women in leadership roles have had to adopt the "strongman" approach to running their teams and organizations. It's considered the gold standard for being a leader.

And yet, I've found that one of the most important keys to unlocking truly great leadership is, in a way, quite the opposite of the John Wayne mentality: vulnerability. That's right. I'm talking about the willingness to open up, show your cards, take advice, admit your mistakes, and make yourself vulnerable to others. This is the kind of behavior that might make John Wayne roll over in his grave, but in my experience, I've found that the willingness to be vulnerable is the key to unlocking truly great leadership.

This dimension of Intelligent Leadership presents a kind of paradox that many leaders don't understand, but that the greatest leaders are intimately familiar with: vulnerability doesn't make you weak, as the John Waynes of the world might believe. Vulnerability will actually make you stronger. It will open you up to new possibilities for yourself and your team that you would never have thought possible. It will build trust among your team members. And perhaps counterintuitively, it can make you *in*vulnerable to so many of the slings and arrows of running a team, company, or organization.

I don't mean to suggest that the John Wayne leadership mentality is entirely off base. There are, indeed, many elements of the tough-guy approach that are important to strong leadership. There's a time, for instance, when leaders need to be able to stand alone, to trust in their own instincts, and act in a direct opposition to those around them. Yet vulnerability, when used appropriately, is a powerful tool that even the toughest individuals can leverage to make themselves even stronger leaders and human beings. I'm not talking about the kind of vulnerability that happens *to* you: buckling in the face of pressure or being caught off guard by an unexpected problem or crisis. No, what I am talking about is opening up intentionally. That's why I call this dimension of the IL code "the vulnerability *decision*." It's a conscious choice that you, as a leader, make to humble yourself, invite feedback from others, and search for answers that you don't already have.

MAKING THE CHOICE TO BE VULNERABLE

I have to admit something. I've played a little trick on you. While thinking differently, thinking big is the *first* dimension of the Intelligent Leadership process, the vulnerability decision is the most *important*. So why do I put it second? Thinking differently, thinking big is a sexier concept, and one that more people tend to associate with great leadership. It has more sizzle, and doesn't seem to intimidate leaders the way vulnerability does. Thinking differently, thinking big helps draw you in to the whole Intelligent Leadership change process, and understand the potential it has to be a truly revolutionary force in your life. Plus, it helps you to establish a big vision for the kind of leader you want to become.

But it's with the vulnerability decision that the rubber really meets the road. Nearly every one of the executives I work with finds this to be the most powerful aspect of our work together. They tend to come from the John Wayne school of leadership, and are under the often-unconscious assumption that vulnerability equals weakness. They've gotten where they are in their careers, which for most of them is quite far, without much, if any, vulnerability. They've survived—and thrived—in the cutthroat world of business and have the titles—and battle scars—to prove it.

But nearly all the executives I work with have become stalled in their development, and need something new to take the next step. That next step is almost always unlocked through making the choice to be vulnerable—with me, with their peer network, and ultimately with themselves. It's how the process of transformation begins. Vulnerability "softens" people and opens them up to the possibility of change. And at the end of their journey, the majority of those I work with credit vulnerability with being the most difficult and yet important step in helping them to take their leadership to the next level.

Now, let's take some time to explore the various dimensions of the vulnerability decision and how you can start to put it into practice in your own life.

THE GATEWAY TO CHANGE

"Without vulnerability, change isn't possible." It's a bold statement, but true, made by a colleague of mine named Curtis Smith, a former Navy man who now runs a corporate consulting firm in Ohio. He's intimately familiar with the John Wayne approach to leadership, through both his own experience in the military and also his current work with corporate management. And he's intimately familiar with its limitations. Companies come to Curtis looking to evolve in some way, and he's found, as I have, that for any change efforts to actually work, vulnerability is the first step.

One of the key components of vulnerability is humility, or the acknowledgment that you don't have all the answers yourself. This can be a tough one for leaders, who often have pretty big egos. But if you want to change yourself or your company, you need to muster enough humility to see and acknowledge that you aren't perfect, and that there are elements of your personality, behavior, management style, or company culture that need improvement. That takes vulnerability.

The problem is that change doesn't necessarily come naturally to us, at least as adults. Children, on the other hand, are like change machines. They are in a rapid state of growth—physically, emotionally, and intellectually. Think about it. If you haven't seen a child in six months or a year, you expect that they will have changed significantly. But it's different for adults. If you see a family member or friend after two years without contact and find that not much has changed, it wouldn't be a big surprise. We're not really expected to change after a certain age. In fact, the average human brain reaches full maturity around the age of twenty-five. Our neural pathways become less malleable and more rigid. This is the time of life that we're expected to get a job, choose a career, start a family, settle down, and generally "grow up." And for most adults, this is the time that we tend to stop actively developing. We become rigid, often out of necessity or convenience, and develop a kind of "comfort zone" that we seldom disrupt.

The vulnerability decision is meant to disrupt that comfort zone and open us up to the possibility of change. When we make ourselves vulnerable to others, we actively dismantle the rigid walls we've built around ourselves, we begin to loosen our fixed ideas about what is possible, and we open ourselves to the territory beyond our comfort zones.

Of course, I'm not suggesting that we revert to childlike behavior. That would be naïve, counterproductive, and dangerous. But in our effort to make ourselves more vulnerable, there is much to be learned from connecting with that part of our own lives when change was a naturally occurring event.

Humility Is Rare

We've studied thousands of individuals through the Mattone Leadership Enneagram Inventory (MLEI), which measures the strength and maturity of a variety of personality traits in those who take the assessment. Our subjects tend to self-select as leaders or aspiring leaders, and so the data we've collected over the years has shown us patterns in the "psychograph" of leaders. In studying these patterns, we've been able to identify the specific traits in which leaders tend to be either stronger or weaker.

One pattern we've identified as a general weakness among leaders is in the Helper trait. This trait is characterized by a strong orientation toward empathizing with and assisting others. Leaders who have a strong expression of this trait tend to place the needs of others and the greater whole above their own. In the most mature examples, this leads to a kind of humility.

But among the leaders we've studied (over 10,000 people have taken the MLEI), we've found the Helper to be the least common, and weakest of all the traits. Leaders and aspiring leaders, it turns out, don't tend to express a high degree of empathy and "other-orientation." Instead, we've found a lot of immature expressions of this trait, where people might do things to help others, but always with a kind of hidden agenda— an expectation of something in return.

The good news is that while this trait is usually underdeveloped, it has a tremendous amount of leverage. When the leaders I've worked with have focused on strengthening this trait, it has had an exponential impact on every other part of their lives. They find that when they can access a truly altruistic motive to help others, all of their other capacities are accentuated in service of this goal. It is often this trait, more than anything else, that unlocks a leader's true potential.

If you want to find out the strength of your own Helper trait, and explore the other dimensions of the MLEI, you can take the assessment for free at johnmattone.com/booktools.

VULNERABILITY AND THE BOTTOM LINE

Curtis Smith, whom we discussed earlier, shared a story with me that not only highlights the importance of vulnerability in the change process, but also points to how it can have a significant impact on the bottom line of an organization. Curtis was hired by a particularly John Wayne–like executive—we will call him Mark—to help him through a difficult transition at the financial technology company he founded and managed. The company was going through a challenging growth phase in which more and more was being demanded of Mark, and it was clear to him that he needed to restructure in order to delegate more responsibility to the next layer of management. So he brought in Curtis to help him.

It didn't take long for Curtis to diagnose the problem—and, unlike Mark had hoped, it wasn't necessarily an organizational fix that his company needed. It was a personal one. Like so many companies that are built on the blood, sweat, and tears of a passionate founder, the underlying problem for Mark was that he didn't want to let go of power and control. The company was his baby, after all; he had founded it and been responsible for nearly every element of its day-to-day operations for years. Whether he was aware of it or not, Mark had an underlying assumption that no one would do as good a job as he, so he might as well do everything himself. And that was creating a massive bottleneck to the growth of the company.

Curtis tried to get Mark to face this reality, but after several months of working together, they were getting nowhere. Mark wouldn't open up to him. He had spent his life seeing vulnerability as weakness, and wasn't about to change that now. In fact, the only value Mark saw in vulnerability was capitalizing on that trait in others in order to take advantage of them and get ahead. Curtis and Mark were at an impasse.

On the edge of giving up, Curtis had an idea. He shared with Mark a story about Jack Welch, the chairman and CEO of General Electric from 1981 to 2001, who is considered one of the most successful executives in American history. During the 1990s, GE, like many companies, was struggling to adapt to the new reality being brought about by the growth and pervasiveness of the internet. Welch recognized that most of the members of his senior management team were older and were less facile in the emerging internet world. So he decided to set up a mass experiment in group vulnerability.

He called it "reverse mentoring." He paired up younger, more internet-adept employees with older members of senior management so that the former could teach the latter about new technologies. The program was a huge success. The "upward" mentoring helped to instill a deeper understanding of web-based technologies among senior management, which was crucial for them to stay ahead in the rapidly changing technological landscape of the time. In the process, strong bonds were developed between the two generations, which helped to facilitate a natural kind of "downward" mentorship. This led to a massive increase in internal promotions.

Mark changed his mind when he heard Welch's story. Hearing this example of one of the most powerful CEOs on earth opening up and admitting that neither he nor his senior management team were equipped to handle the next step in their company's evolution, and then humbling themselves to their junior staff in order to address the situation, had a big impact on Mark. It was a concrete example of how vulnerability could actually make him and his company stronger, and it gave him a kind of permission to follow Welch's lead. Mark started to let go more at work, and open himself up to restructuring the company in a way that would take more responsibility off his shoulders and set up the company for growth. As a result of his vulnerability decision, and his subsequent receptivity to a multitude of changes, his company doubled in size in the next six months.

Vulnerability, it turns out, not only makes you a stronger leader. It can lead to very real, concrete results for you and your organization!

ADMITTING YOUR FLAWS BUILDS TRUST

One of the key components of the vulnerability decision is the willingness to openly acknowledge and then embrace your flaws. This can be very difficult because, again, many leaders perceive this as a kind of weakness. They believe this will make them seem fallible, and thus they will lose their authority and respect. But if done in the right way, being open about one's imperfections has the opposite effect, and the best leaders know how to do this.

Admitting your flaws accomplishes several goals. First, it allows you to admit that there is room for improvement. How can you change if you think you're already perfect? If you can get past yourself and see that you—as a human being and a leader—are more of a work-in-progress than you are a final product, then you'll set the stage to make the kind of changes necessary to take yourself—and your team—to the next level.

Second, being transparent about your imperfections inspires a tremendous sense of trust in you from your team. The truth is that those who work with and for you already know that you're not perfect. Funnily enough, they are likely more intimately familiar with your imperfections than you are. When you openly admit your imperfections, it communicates that you are self-aware. This puts people at ease. No one expects perfection, and if your colleagues and staff know that you are conscious of your gaps, they can more fully trust that you'll take responsibility for them. It may sound counterintuitive, but it works.

This is as true at a company level as it is on a personal level. Take Anne Mulcahy, the former CEO of Xerox, for example. When Mulcahy took over Xerox in 2000, the company was in dire straits. Their business model had become unsustainable, with expenses too high and profit margins too low. As a primarily paper-based business, they were struggling to adapt to the increasingly digital world. Shareholders were losing confidence and the stock price had dropped 26 points. The company was on the verge of bankruptcy.

Rather than keep these fundamental issues under wraps for fear of undermining her own authority, she chose to engage in an act of supreme vulnerability. Mulcahy met personally with Xerox's top one hundred executives, being very transparent about the dire nature of the company's position, and asking for their support in helping to "restore Xerox to a great company again." It was a risky move, but Mulcahy decided it would be more credible and authoritative if she acknowledged that the company was broken and that nothing short of dramatic actions would fix it. All but two executives chose to stay on board through the transition, and most are still with the company to this day. Those brave leaders were crucial in engineering Xerox's ultimately successful reinvention.

Mulcahy didn't limit her transparency only to her management team. She initiated a campaign to address as many of their customers' complaints as possible, saying, "I will fly anywhere to save any customer for Xerox." And she did. By communicating so transparently to their customer base, she opened herself up to feedback, much of which was very difficult to hear. But it worked. She gained the trust of her customers by involving them in Xerox's reinvention process, and received valuable information about their concerns and future needs that she and her team used to transform the company.

It didn't take long for Mulcahy to turn Xerox around. With valuable support from her customers and leadership team—support that she invited and cultivated—she was able to restore the company's greatness and transform the business model for the twenty-first century.

CREATING A CULTURE OF VULNERABILITY

In my 2016 book, *Cultural Transformations*, I interviewed fourteen of today's most respected CEOs about the role that culture plays in their organizations. Culture, in my definition, is the sum total of the shared values and directives—spoken and implicit—of any group. It's an invisible matrix of relationships that binds people together and animates their work and behavior. One of the key insights from all of the CEOs I interviewed was the direct correlation between leadership and the culture of an organization. It's literally one to one. You, as a leader, will set the tone for your company's culture. You model the behavior and attitudes for everyone, which is an enormous responsibility.

Vulnerability is one of the biggest leverage points between you, the leader, and the culture of your organization. One of the most impressive CEOs I interviewed for *Cultural Transformations* was Kris Canekeratne, chairman and CEO of an IT services company called Virtusa, who said the following about vulnerability:

> We can learn a lot from mistakes, whether in life or at work. I think what's important is to make sure that the same mistakes don't happen again, that you learn from and institutionalize them so the organization can evolve. I have found that when things don't work well, looking in the mirror and reflecting deeply on what I could have done better or differently is a terrific exercise. This is easier said than done, because strong individuals often feel that failure was not theirs but someone else's. But I believe that the best, most able leaders first look at themselves. They introspect and try to learn from their mistakes. They're willing to accept the fact that they erred. Being able to confront and acknowledge one's mistakes transmits one of the most important of all leadership tenets, humility. This further strengthens the trust between leaders and their team members.

This issue of trust is key. Trust is a fundamental building block of a strong organizational culture. And like we discussed above, by being vulnerable and transparent with others, you make it possible for them to trust you. In fact, my colleague Lyne Cathcart, a Quebec-based executive coach, has found vulnerability to be contagious. When she works with CEOs, she has them do interviews with the key stakeholders within their companies, asking for feedback and input. She says that they are hesitant at first, fearing that such behavior might lessen their power. One client even said, "You're asking me to open my kimono in front of my employees."

But when they follow through, Cathcart's clients find that their employees respond surprisingly well, feeling privileged to be given the opportunity to share feedback with their boss. In fact, the CEOs' vulnerability creates a sense of admiration and awe in those they open up to. The staff are impressed by the courage it takes for the leader to humble herself in that way, and it inspires them to do the same. A culture of vulnerability is created—one in which people are unafraid of their imperfection, are open to communication, and are always striving to improve, individually and collectively.

Don't Wait

In the last chapter, I shared with you the story of my encounter with Apple cofounder Steve Jobs. In my work with Steve, I could tell—and he essentially said as much—that he had a sense of regret over leaving until so late in his life the kind of self-reflection we were doing together. At that point, he had already been diagnosed with pancreatic cancer, and knew that his days were limited. He wanted to use the time he had left to make sure that his relationships and his legacy were in the best shape possible. And he knew he couldn't do that alone, or without going deep. Toward the end of our sessions, he expressed that he was grateful for the work we did together, and wished that he had done this kind of inquiry much earlier in his career. He could have done a lot more good in the world, and avoided some of the mistakes that cost him dearly, both professionally and personally.

Unfortunately, Jobs's late-in-life vulnerability is all too common. Most of the leaders I work with are in the tail end of their careers, and nearly all of them express to me that they wished they had started their journeys of introspection and vulnerability much earlier.

I don't bring this up to create a sense of regret. I do it to create a sense of urgency. There is no time like the present to make your own vulnerability decision. And it's never too late. The information about yourself that you can discover through asking for input, and the kind of trust that you can build through your own vulnerability, can set the stage for a long and rewarding journey that will maximize your potential as a leader. The sooner you do it, the farther you'll be able to go.

CAN YOU BE TOO HUMBLE?

Like the other dimensions of Intelligent Leadership, there can be a downside to vulnerability. In the attempt to humble yourself, you can take things too far and, in the process, undermine your own confidence. And you can't afford to lose confidence. It is absolutely crucial to good leadership.

One of my recent clients reported that after a week of working with me on vulnerability—reaching out to co-workers and peers for feedback—he was experiencing a significant lack of confidence. "I just feel self-conscious and weak," he told me. The brazen, my-way-or-the-highway belief in himself that had carried him this far in life didn't jive with the more vulnerable approach, and he wasn't able to reconcile the two in himself. I told him that he needed to take a lighter approach—not to throw the baby out with the bathwater. He was the same person with all the same qualities he'd always had. He was just inviting more people into his world. That perspective allowed him to hold both qualities at the same time—confidence and vulnerability.

This is a common overcorrection for those who begin to make themselves more vulnerable. I have noticed a similar tendency among many of the leaders I work with. They tend to overshoot the target. In fact, they often find that when they seek feedback from others, their own opinion of themselves is much lower than the opinion of those they reach out to. They are much more fixated with their flaws than those around them. In their attempts to embrace their imperfections, they tend to focus too much on their negative aspects, while overlooking some of the valuable traits that make them leaders in the first place. This overly negative sense of self can be the flip side of the John Wayne mentality. If you haven't had a lot of experience with this kind of conscious vulnerability, it's common to overreact in the face of your imperfections and it can be difficult to maintain a sense of confidence in spite of them.

So it's important to have a balanced and nuanced approach to vulnerability. We don't want to be John Wayne, but we don't want to be Eeyore either, focusing too much on the negatives and allowing ourselves to lose confidence. We want to find that compelling balance of strength and humility that all the greatest leaders have. This may sound impossible, but it's not. We will explore how to strike this balance of embracing the best and worst parts of yourself while maintaining an abiding sense of confidence when we get to Chapter 5, "Leveraging Your Gifts and Addressing Your Gaps."

PRACTICING VULNERABILITY

As we've been discussing, vulnerability is neither easy nor common. In my experience, vulnerability takes practice. It's not something you can just "get" and then be done. *In*vulnerability tends to be a kind of default setting for most of us. If we're not constantly chipping away at the walls we build around ourselves, then it will be very difficult for us to put this dimension of Intelligent Leadership into practice.

Below are a series of "igniter behaviors" that you can use to cultivate vulnerability. They are behaviors that you can put into practice right away to help expand the way you think. They are also "leading indicators" of how much you embody this dimension of leadership, and are meant to help you measure yourself so you can determine what areas need improvement.

As you read them, I encourage you to reflect upon how much you do or don't consistently exhibit these behaviors. Once you've gone through them yourself, reach out to your support network and ask them if they agree with your assessment.

Taking the Time to Reflect

It's important to engage in some kind of regular practice of vulnerability, both with yourself and with others. I like to take 15 minutes at the end of each day to reflect on the quality of my actions and interactions. I ask myself if my thoughts and emotions were positive and strong. I assess whether my actions reflected my values and whether I had exhibited strong character.

Once I've reviewed the day, I decide if I like what I'm seeing: Were there things that I could have done differently? This is an exercise in being vulnerable with myself, and puts me in a state of openness to be able to improve moving forward. I've found that this is a strong habit to develop if you want to improve your leadership. There's no set way to do this—you can use any variety of methods for self-reflection. The key is to do something regularly to put yourself in a reflective mindset. The power to change for the better is always ignited paradoxically from connecting *deeply* and *quietly* with the depths of our inner being.

Being Open to Feedback

One of the best ways to reflect on yourself is to seek out feedback from others. You don't have to do this every day, but it's important to take time, occasionally, to make sure that you're connecting to the impact that you're having on those around you. In what ways is your inner world spilling over onto others? Are your actions—which are reflections of your inner core—having a negative or positive effect on your family, friends, and co-workers?

As you reach out, it's very important to cultivate a degree of being open to this feedback from others. Of course, this is difficult, but maintaining openness in the face of feedback is one of the keys to vulnerability. If your mindset is *in*vulnerable, you will never grow. You have the choice either to accept or reject feedback; however, if you reject feedback, you also reject the choice of acting in a way that may very well bring you abundant success and happiness. If you think you can do this journey alone, you are wrong. You need to cultivate an inner circle of trusted people who can help you to become and remain vulnerable.

Being Proactive

When you are trying to cultivate any new quality, it's crucial that you are proactive. This is especially true with vulnerability because, as we've discussed, the idea of being vulnerable can bring up tremendous fear, so actually making yourself vulnerable requires a lot of courage. You can't wait for vulnerability to come to you.

Don't wait for feedback, either internally or externally, to force you into becoming open. It's better to take the offensive. Become an expert in yourself, through reflection and feedback.

CHAPTER 4

Having a Mindset of Entitlement versus a Mindset of Duty

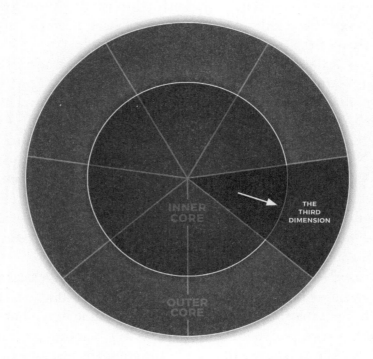

Few of us would argue with the fact that in today's society, especially in the West, there is a ubiquitous presence of an entitlement mentality. Gone are the days when the daily struggle to survive, to put bread on the table, was the way of life for the majority of the population. Instead, we see an ever-increasing number of people with an overinflated sense of their skills and capacities, and a belief that they should get rewarded for simply showing up. The blood, sweat, and tears of earlier generations that laid the foundation for the wealth and prosperity that so many individuals enjoy today are far in the rearview mirror. Being out of touch with what it takes to succeed, and expecting that the privileges that you have are, in fact, not privileges but your God-given right, creates a mindset that can inhibit your ability to work hard through unexpected challenges. And this entitlement mentality is having negative effects everywhere, from the classroom to the boardroom.

The entitlement mentality is fueled, in part, by narcissism, which is on the rise. In her 2009 book, *The Narcissism Epidemic: Living in the Age of Entitlement*, Dr. Jean Twenge, a psychology researcher at San Diego State University, charts the rise of this broad scale sense of self-importance. She compared the results of the Narcissistic Personality Inventory (NPI) conducted in 1982 and 2006, during which over 16,000 subjects answered a series of questions to measure their degree of self-centeredness. It turns out that over this two-decade period, the number of people scoring a significant degree of narcissism on the NPI doubled, going from one in eight to one in four!

Unsurprisingly, both the entitlement mentality and narcissism are permeating the business world. Workers are seeking jobs with meaning, and roles where they feel that they can make an impact, and businesses experience the effects of this in their turnover rates. We are no longer living in the days of the company man or woman who gets a job out of college and loyally sticks with that same organization until their retirement. In his 2012 article "Generation Flux," which graced the cover of *Fast Company* magazine, Robert Safian charts a chaotic new business landscape in which it is common for people to change career paths multiple times throughout their working life. What we are seeing is a shifting emphasis from the company to the individual. The members of Generation Flux are looking for jobs and companies that will help them to thrive and succeed as individuals; and are more likely to move on to new opportunities if they aren't personally satisfied.

This is true not just for employees, but for executives as well. In their paper for *Administrative Science Quarterly,* "It's All About Me: Narcissistic CEOs and Their Effects on Company Strategy and Performance," Penn State University professors Arijit Chatterjee and Donald C. Hambrick suggest that narcissism is on the rise in the executive suite. "Three decades ago," says Hambrick, "the typical CEO was likely to be a Steady Eddie, CEO as steward, who would hold the organization together, want to leave it in good shape, deliver satisfactorily for all parties involved. Contemporary CEOs are much more likely to be risk-takers who are flamboyant and colorful and view themselves as something akin to celebrities." It's true. A nominal review of business news will show just how likely CEOs are to leave one company for the next bigger and brighter opportunity. In other words, they're more in it for themselves than they are dedicated to their organization.

I have to say that this is, in part, my fault. I'm a baby boomer after all. We were the original "Me Generation"—the ones who sparked the self-esteem revolution, breaking free from the shackles of tradition and institutions, and elevating the importance of the individual to an all-time high. But before you get the impression that I'm old-fashioned and yearning for some bygone era when people worked for the same company their whole life, let me tell you that I'm not. I see the rise of individual empowerment as an incredibly positive development for society. It gives us the freedom to explore our potential and lead more fulfilling, self-actualized lives. It's just that alongside this rise in individual empowerment, we've naturally started to lose sight of something that is crucial to great leadership: a sense of interconnectedness and privileged duty to something beyond ourselves.

I've found that the best leaders, while expressing a high degree of individual empowerment, are deeply beholden to a larger whole, whether that be their family, their organization, their country, the whole planet, or all of the above. This mindset of duty is very different than believing that the world owes you something, and that you are entitled to certain privileges or advantages regardless of your actions. Those beliefs will inevitably lead you to act in ways that will (perhaps unintentionally) undermine the success of any project that you are a part of. Leaders, true leaders, are not entitled, but instead are driven by a sense of service to a greater community—a sense of duty to something more significant than themselves. If you can embrace this duty mindset, then you will embody the kind of broader perspective that leaders need to guide the evolution of any organization.

You may have noticed that I'm using the word "mindset" when I describe these different motives driving leaders. I define "mindset" as the perspective through which you're seeing yourself and the world. It's the foundation of your behavior, and is shaped by your inner core beliefs and values. That's why I call the third dimension of Intelligent Leadership "Having a Mindset of Entitlement versus a Mindset of Duty." The keyword here is mindset. It's important to be clear about your own mindset as you embark on the journey of developing as a leader, especially if you want to succeed.

Granted, there are plenty of well-known and very successful leaders out there who seem to be acting primarily for their own betterment: They are clearly driven by the desire for fame, wealth, or power. But the *greatest* of leaders—the ones who have had a truly lasting impact on the people around them—exhibit a significant degree of duty to the causes and people they've served. How this sense of duty manifests is often subtle, and can be hard to see, but when you observe these leaders closely over the long term, you'll see what's really driving them. You'll be able to determine, from their behavior over time, just who they are serving: themselves, or the greater whole.

We'll spend the rest of this chapter exploring your mindset, your level of entitlement, and the power that having a duty mindset can have in unlocking your potential as a leader.

SEEING THROUGH YOUR ENTITLEMENT

Many people with whom I work do not immediately see the value in this dimension of Intelligent Leadership. After all, few people tend to see themselves as "entitled," especially those with more life experience and accumulated wisdom. Entitlement, they often think, is a problem with the younger generations. *They're the ones who don't understand how lucky they are and seem to be too "in it for themselves."* But before you quickly assume that you already understand what duty means, and aren't victim to the entitlement mentality, I encourage you to take a deeper look. This dimension of Intelligent Leadership is very subtle. Even the most altruistic, dutiful among us can have invisible layers of entitlement that, if seen through, can further liberate our leadership potential.

In my experience, all of us live with a certain baseline entitlement. It's human nature to think primarily of yourself and your own needs, and to overlook many of the people and circumstances that have contributed to your own success in life. Even if you're one of those rare individuals who was given next to nothing in your life and have had to earn every advantage you have, there is probably someone else out there who has been given less and had to work harder than you. The key with this dimension isn't to assume that you're not entitled; it's to find the subtle ways in which you may be holding a mindset of entitlement that, if brought to light, might make you an even more conscious, altruistic, and powerful leader.

To help you uncover your own entitlement, let's do a little exercise. I want you to think about the various dimensions of your life: your family, your work, your home, your friendships, your level of wealth, your reputation. Do you feel grateful for them? Do you feel as if you deserve more? Do you feel that the current level of happiness or success you have in all these dimensions is the accurate result of the life you've lived and the kind of person you are?

Now take this a little deeper. Think about your "lot in life." What kind of life were you born into? Were you born rich or poor? What about the time, or era, during which you were born? Do you feel grateful to be alive at this time in human history? What kind of opportunities have you been given along the way? How much of the success that you've experienced in your life can be traced to forces that were out of your control?

Even if you are a rare individual who was given next to nothing and made the best of it, there have likely been big breaks that have helped you along the way. Maybe you had a mentor or teacher or coach who believed in you when no one else would. Maybe you had an extremely supportive parent who sacrificed a tremendous amount to give you more opportunities.

As you think through the forces that have led to the life you're living, can you feel a shift in your perspective? Are you starting to get a sense of how much you take for granted?

As you begin to see through your own layers of entitlement, no matter how gross or subtle they are, you may begin to feel a natural sense of gratitude for and obligation to the people and circumstances that have led to where you are.

Many people who do this exercise feel two things simultaneously. First, they start to see themselves as benefiting from billions of little choices and circumstances, including everything from being born into their particular family to where they chose to attend college. They see that they are the beneficiaries not only of their own choices, but also of the choices made by others on their behalf. They begin to experience themselves with a longer-term view, one that is connected backward in time, and they feel the forward momentum of their own life, almost like riding a wave made up of all these choices and circumstances.

Secondly, people begin to see their lives from a broader context. Their awareness expands, as if they've been lifted out of the small problems and responsibilities of their personal lives, and are looking down on themselves from a 60,000-foot view. From this vantage point, they can see themselves as part of a much bigger life process, and perceive the crucial role they play in that process. Sometimes this shows up as people recognizing their responsibility for others—family members, kids, or coworkers or employees. Sometimes people see that they are in a position to make an intellectual, or political, or philosophical contribution to society. Regardless of the specifics, in this exercise, people often become aware of the interconnectedness of their own lives and actions with the broader fabric of society. It is ironic, isn't it, that as people look beyond their own self-obsession, they start to feel an even greater significance in their own lives? Their sense of significance is no longer based on an arbitrary sense of self-importance, but now on a felt sense of obligation to the people and environment around them that is part of who they are and how they got to be where they are now.

Can you feel these elements begin to emerge in your own perspective? That's the duty mindset, and found almost instantaneously upon seeing through your Entitlement mentality. Let's explore it further.

Measuring Your Narcissism

In Chapter 1, I introduced you to the Mattone Leadership Enneagram Inventory (MLEI), which is an assessment I've developed to help measure your own leadership style and maturity. Over the years, thousands of leaders and aspiring leaders have taken the MLEI, and I've found that a significant majority have scored highly in the areas of both self-confidence (on the positive side) but also self-centeredness (on the negative, flip side). This is only natural. Many people who find themselves in a position of leadership have a high self-concept. It's often a big part of what vaults them into leadership positions.

By learning to understand the various dimensions of their leadership style and maturity through taking the MLEI, leaders are able to get a fuller picture of both the positive and negative aspects of themselves. From here they can better learn to address their gaps and leverage their strengths (as we'll discuss further in the next chapter).

If you'd like to get a better sense of your own level of self-confidence and self-centeredness, along with your other leadership qualities, I encourage you to take the assessment online: johnmattone.com/booktools.

THE DUTY MINDSET: CONTEXT IS EVERYTHING

When I speak about "duty," I don't mean a blind adherence or obligation to a creed or group. I'm talking about a *mindset* of duty. This is a much more dynamic and consciously chosen kind of duty. It's all about seeing yourself in context. The duty mindset is a perspective in which you see yourself as a key cog in a much larger wheel. This wheel is defined by the intricate matrix of relationships that make up who you are: with your co-workers, your family, your friends, your superiors, as well as your mentors and peers. In this larger context a lot is depending you. You are not just an independent actor or solo operator. Your choices, your behavior, and your actions all really matter—they have consequences on all of the many relationships that make up your life.

The best leaders understand this, and they take action based on it. It doesn't mean that they don't act out of self-interest or on their own behalf. It's just that they see their own self-interest as part of something bigger. It's a kind of "enlightened self-interest" in which you are focused on your "self," but that self represents something much bigger. In that light, the duty mindset inherently reorients all of the personal work you're doing. Your own improvement—your striving to become a better leader—becomes much more about the influence you can have on this complex matrix of relationships than it does on your own personal gain. Of course, if you're seeing yourself in this bigger context, and doing your best to make sure your impact is as big and positive as possible, you will naturally benefit personally. But that's not the goal; it's a side effect.

The best leaders I have worked with never take for granted this obligation to positively impact those around them—their family, employees, the organization they work for, their friends, even society. They are driven by an almost maniacal pursuit to positively touch the hearts, minds, and souls of those around them. It becomes a non-negotiable pursuit. *Because* the best of the best leaders don't ever take this responsibility for granted and *because* their duty is born out of an insatiable desire to be "other-oriented" as opposed to "self-oriented," their noble, authentic intent translates into behaviors and actions that are seen by others as real. This becomes the ultimate positive expression of possessing a duty mindset—the leader is seen by others as being authentic—the "real deal."

In the introduction to the book, I asked you to choose several examples of great leadership that you've encountered in your life. I talked about the "glow" that these leaders have—a kind of elusive quality or "X factor" that is hard to define. I would argue that the duty mindset is a big part of this great leadership glow. The best leaders understand, embrace, internalize, and embody this dedication to a larger cause or whole and possess an implicit self-awareness that they are an example for others to follow. This gives them a natural dignity that is compelling. In any group situation, the person who is paying attention to the biggest picture and acting on behalf of the largest whole will likely stand out and be a natural attractor to everyone else.

This is the very definition of what it takes to be a positive role model. When you become more interested in the well-being of the whole than you are in yourself, you become a "magnet" that attracts positive energy and vitality from others. The "glow" from a leader ignites "glow" in and from others. Remember our crystal metaphor from Chapter 1? A beautiful crystal will always reflect beautiful, colorful patterns of light. Great leaders create great families, great organizations, great governments, great societies, and a great world *because* of their "glow" and the "glow" they ignite in others.

FROM SETBACK TO OPPORTUNITY: OVERCOMING THE VICTIM MENTALITY

One of the most powerful aspects of the duty mindset is how it enables you to deal with challenging situations. When your attitude toward life tends to be colored primarily by an entitlement mentality, you're more likely to respond to setbacks by feeling victimized. Something bad has happened *to you*. If you believe the world "owes you" something or that you're entitled to a certain degree of success, you're going to be ill-equipped to respond creatively and positively to the inevitable setbacks that life sends your way. But if you're embracing and living the duty mindset, you're more likely to see setbacks as a natural part of the process. You understand that dealing with curveballs is an inherent part of your role as a leader, not to mention your continued growth as a leader. From this vantage point, you're able to see the "silver linings" in negative situations, find creative solutions, and—as the old saying goes—turn lemons into lemonade.

You are also able to stay laser-focused on the "present" as opposed to getting distracted and pulled in directions that inhibit you from solving problems. When you feel overwhelmed with all the stimuli barraging you in your business and your life, just remind yourself that the journey you are on is a *privileged* one and that your own journey is *less about you* and much *more about* the success and abundance you can bring to others. It's amazing that sometimes making this subtle mindset shift allows you to fully absorb, appreciate, and then successfully navigate the challenges right in front of you. The absolute best leaders I have ever coached have demonstrated an incredible ability to focus on the present, which I believe was fueled by this duty mindset.

Take, for example, Nabil Al Alawi, who is the founder and CEO of Al Mansoori Specialized Engineering, a major player in the Middle Eastern oil and gas industry. Nabil may be the least "victimized" person I've ever met, and his nonvictimized stance had a big impact on his success as an entrepreneur and CEO. When I interviewed Nabil for my last book, *Cultural Transformations*, I asked him what he considered to be the key to his success. His answer was simple: "Maintaining an optimistic attitude in the face of adversity."

The son of Yemeni immigrants, Nabil grew up in both Singapore and Egypt, eventually earning a scholarship to Louisiana

State University, where he got a degree in engineering. He built, from the ground up, an energy company that now does business in twenty-four countries in the Middle East. Nabil has been handed very little in his life or career, and he's worked for every privilege that he now enjoys.

Nabil has had to overcome his share of challenges, both in his personal life and his career. But none may be bigger than his cancer diagnosis. When Nabil was diagnosed with cancer in 2002, he didn't respond to the situation by feeling victimized. Nabil realized that he wouldn't be able to cure himself of the disease if he didn't address the entire lifestyle that, for him, had contributed to his cancer. He attacked his cancer through a combination of conventional treatments and lifestyle adjustments (nutrition, stress, etc.); and was ultimately successful.

As a result of his cancer journey, Nabil realized that he could be doing more to support a healthy lifestyle for his company employees. He initiated a comprehensive shift in his company's priorities. Rather than focusing merely on the financial bottom line as the key indicator of his company's success, Nabil now also looks at the health of his employees. Al Mansoori is dedicated to supporting a lifestyle that reduces stress, promotes healthy living practices, and provides top-notch health care for all its employees. And it's been a huge success. Al Mansoori has become a model for corporate health programs and has record levels of employee satisfaction, all while enjoying continued financial growth over the past decade. And their example and success has started to rub off on their clients. Inspired by Nabil's health program, Shell, Exxon, and BP are all beginning to implement similar initiatives.

Had Nabil perceived his cancer diagnosis as an affront to the life he felt he *deserved*, he never would have found the wherewithal to respond in the way he did. Like so many great leaders, he saw within his personal crisis an opportunity to make life better for the many people to whom he felt a duty.

THE FIRST THREE DIMENSIONS: A PACKAGE DEAL

At this point, you may be starting to see the ways in which the various dimensions of Intelligent Leadership work together. In fact, thinking differently, thinking big and the vulnerability decision both have a significant influence on cultivating a duty mindset, and vice versa.

For example, if you're attempting to see through your own entitlement (the third dimension), it's crucial that you are able to be vulnerable with yourself and others (the second dimension). And the opposite is also true. Understanding the implicit obligation that you, as a leader, have to all the dimensions in your life helps to create a kind of vulnerability. You realize just how dependent you are on others.

Thinking differently, thinking big (the first dimension) is also deeply connected to the duty mindset (the third dimension). In fact, learning to see yourself in a larger context is a powerful form of thinking big. As you may remember from that chapter, the most direct way to access thinking differently, thinking big is to get clear about your core purpose. And learning to see yourself and your life in the biggest possible context, as you do with the duty mindset, is an invaluable way to start to perceive your core purpose.

As you continue to make your way through Intelligent Leadership, I encourage you to continue looking for the many ways that the dimensions overlap and support one another. They're designed that way, and the more you can perceive these synergies, the more powerful will be your understanding of Intelligent Leadership.

DON'T FORGET TO PUT ON YOUR OWN OXYGEN MASK FIRST

Like the other dimensions of Intelligent Leadership, there are drawbacks and potential dangers associated with the duty mindset. It's important that in your attempts to see through your own entitlement, you don't go too far in the opposite direction and undermine your sense of self-worth. Having a high degree of personal confidence is a very important component of good leadership. In fact, it's probably carried you pretty far in your life. Believing in yourself allows you to stand up to criticism, overcome obstacles, and inspire others. The key is to find the right balance, so your self-esteem doesn't get out of control and cloud your ability to understand the obligation you have to the greater whole.

If you've ever actually paid attention to the safety speech given by flight attendants, you might recall their instructions to put on your own oxygen mask first in case of emergency. You need to make sure that you are healthy and safe in order to then help out those around you. I tend to think of the relationship between the individual and the whole when it comes to the duty mindset as similar to this safety paradox. As a leader, your primary obligation is to the many "wholes" in your life that you are a part of. You have a duty to serve and support them. But in order to be a great "Intelligent Leader," you have to also make sure that you, personally, are strong and supportive.

To further illustrate this point, I'd like to introduce the concept of a "holon," which is a Greek term made popular by the futurist Arthur Koestler in his 1967 book, *The Ghost in the Machine*. Koestler describes a holon as a unit that is both whole unto itself, but also part of a larger whole. That's how I like to think of the ideal relationship between you, the individual leader, and the many wholes that you are a part of. In perceiving your duty and obligation to the organizations, families, and companies you are a part of, you must always maintain your own strength as an individual. You are the most important "whole" in your own life, and if you want to be of service to others, it's crucial that you are strong and vibrant.

Finally, as you seek the duty mindset, remember not to revert to more mechanical forms of duty. The duty mindset doesn't mean blindly dedicating yourself to a principle or organization. You should never "turn off" your critical thinking or practice loyalty for loyalty's sake. As we discussed earlier in the chapter, the duty mindset is more about seeing the many ways in which you are deeply connected to and responsible for the matrix of relation-ships in your life. How you choose to act on that sense of obliga-tion is entirely up to you!

CULTIVATING A DUTY MINDSET

Great leaders make the duty mindset look natural. When you're in the presence of someone who is looking out for the whole and possesses a deep degree of altruism, it can often feel as if they were born that way. But in my experience, for most of us, the duty mindset is something that we need to work on. We have a natural tendency toward self-obsession that takes effort to override. Even the saintliest among us can go even further in their ability to see themselves in a bigger context. To me, this is good news! It means that we can all improve from where we are right now.

Below are a series of "igniter behaviors" for the duty mind-set. These are actions that you can take to help expand your own perspective. The idea is that the more you are able to man-ually apply these behaviors, the more they will become second nature to you—an inherent part of the way you see yourself and the world.

As you work through them, take the time to reflect on how each of them affects your worldview. Do you feel a greater sense of awareness? Are you less preoccupied with yourself and more focused on others?

Working Backward Exercise

At least once per month take stock of all your successes—all the good things that have happened to you and all those situations that led to your feeling proud, happy, and fulfilled. Now create four columns, and list your successes, one by one, on the left. In the next column, write down the positive result that you experienced from each success. Make sure to be specific and provide details. For example, if you were fortunate enough to earn a bonus, write down how much the bonus was for. In the next column, write down what you, personally, did that led to your success. With the bonus example, for instance, did you take on more responsibility to earn it? In the next column, write down the names of everyone who made some kind of contribution that led to your success. These could be individuals with whom you work, as well as others, like family, friends, or past colleagues. For example, maybe your spouse spent more time with your kids to enable you to put in the extra work that led to your bonus. In the last column, write down your reaction to seeing that your success was the result of more than just your own effort (if that was the case).

This exercise is a powerful way to experience being other-oriented as opposed to self-oriented (entitled and selfish), and to see how it is a key ingredient to achievement, success, and good leadership. Once you see that you are actually a small part of a much bigger whole, it keeps you humble, which allows you to better appreciate all the value that others bring to your own success.

Becoming Trustworthy

One of the most important elements of the duty mindset is being the kind of person that others can count on, because you know they are counting on you. It's kind of a chicken-and-egg situation. The more awake you are to how many people you're connected to, the more incentive you have to be a trustworthy person. And the more trustworthy you are, the more you'll start to wake up to just how many people are counting on you. You'll, in turn, start to trust others more because you realize just how interdependent we all are. Just like in the exercise above, you can see that you need others to succeed and they need you. And trust is the key to making all of that work.

So ask yourself, are you a trusting person? And are you a trustworthy person? Why or why not? Did the "walking backward" exercise above inspire you to become more trustworthy? Take some time to reflect on this, and consider checking in with your board of directors to see how they view you in this regard. Are you the kind of person people put their faith in?

Taking Pride in Others

Pride is a double-edged sword. On one hand, it can lead to arrogance and stubbornness, and make you hard to work with. On the other, it can be a natural result of having done a good job or achieved something through hard work and dedication. When it comes to the duty mindset, it's taking pride in others, not ourselves, that we're most interested in. As you start to see yourself in a bigger and bigger context, the more you start to identify with that bigger whole. Consequently, you'll start to take pride in it. Think of your family. When your children accomplish something, it makes you proud. The same goes for a team you're a part of. I would argue that pride in a collective effort is far more powerful and fulfilling than personal pride (as important as that may be).

Take some time to consider the "greater wholes" that make you proud. Are there specific accomplishments that have been achieved by others who are part of your group or by the group itself that have made you proud? How does that feeling of pride compare to your own personal pride? Just taking the time to reflect on this greater sense of pride starts to build the muscles of your duty mindset.

CHAPTER 5

Leveraging Your Gifts and Addressing Your Gaps

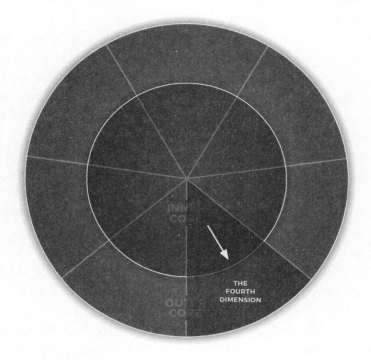

When I was in college, my friend Tony and I spent our spring break on a backpacking trip in the Escalante River wilderness in southern Utah. It was a five-day adventure through one of the country's most beautiful—and desolate—regions, characterized by striking red rock desert landscapes with scarce water and unrelenting sun inhabited by only the most resilient of plants and animals.

To survive our journey, we had to carry all the essentials—food, water, shelter—on our backs. We spent months preparing, making countless trips to the local outdoor gear store to make sure we had what we needed: tents, sleeping pads, cooking stove, pots and pans, water purifiers. We packed everything.

Everything, that is, but a map.

We had a guidebook with some written descriptions of the route, accompanied by some simple sketches of trail branches and landmarks; and in our youthful arrogance, we thought that was sufficient. The trip route followed a single, winding river at the bottom of a deep canyon most of the way. Why would we need a map for that?

The problem, as we discovered on day five of what, up until that point, had been an extraordinary trip, was determining just where we were supposed to climb our way out of the canyon in order to take the proper trail back to our car. The Escalante River is a winding maze of sharp, 180-degree curves, nearly every one of which looks the same. So when it was time to figure out just exactly where in this unending string of curves we were supposed to exit, our vague guidebook descriptions were insufficient and left a lot to guesswork.

We, of course, guessed wrong, and exited the canyon twenty miles away from our car. And since we didn't have a map, we didn't know we'd made the wrong decision. All we knew is that we were looking for a road, which we couldn't find. It was 95 degrees, there were no trees to offer shade, and we were draining our water supply quickly. We had filtration pumps, but we needed a source of water. There were plenty of creek beds to be found, but they were all dry as a bone!

As the afternoon progressed, things went from bad to worse. Our water ran out, Tony began to hallucinate from heat exhaustion, and we were no closer to finding the road. I started to panic.

And out in the wilderness, panic can be life-threatening. Just as things were about to get really grim, I caught a glimpse of light out of the corner of my eye. It was the reflection of sun on water—a puddle in an otherwise dry creek bed. Tony and I sprinted down the bank, threw off our backpacks, and feverishly pumped water through our filters. To this day, it remains in my memory as the sweetest drink of water I've ever had.

The rest of the story is, as they say, history. With our hydration-inspired clarity, we were able to climb to a nearby high point and spot a road far off in the distance. From there, we were able to flag down a lone vehicle and hitch a ride back to our car. We survived—barely—in spite of our navigational arrogance, and learned a valuable lesson about the importance of having an accurate map of the territory before beginning any journey.

You may be wondering why I'm telling you this story. Well, the truth is, many of us make the same mistake as Tony and I did, only instead of being unprepared out in the wilderness, we are without a map of the uncharted territory that is our own inner self, the very one that we're embarking upon changing when we decide to engage in the process of leadership development. The map needed for leadership development is not one that someone can just hand over to you. It's not like buying a street atlas at the gas station: Your map will be unique to you. Why? We all have different strengths that we can leverage to become more effective leaders, and we all have particular weaknesses that we need to become aware of and improve upon in order to unleash our potential. So, how are you going to evolve your capacities as a leader? You need a plan. You need a map; you need to know where you are, and where you're trying to go. And in order to develop that plan, it's absolutely crucial that you get clear about your own strengths and weaknesses.

I've worked with hundreds of leaders in a coaching capacity, and you'd be surprised at just how inaccurate are most people's sense of their strengths and weaknesses. There are a lot of reasons for this. Some have never really taken the time to look at what they are good at and what needs improving. They're busy people and don't necessarily see the ROI on this kind of self-assessment. Even if they've thought about it themselves, many have never sought genuine feedback from friends, peers, or family, so their sense of themselves isn't objective. And sometimes, when they have sought feedback from others, those giving it were too shy to be honest, and so they didn't receive an accurate picture.

That's what this dimension of Intelligent Leadership is all about. "Leveraging Your Gifts and Addressing Your Gaps" focuses on helping you get the most accurate possible picture of yourself, and then learning to use that information effectively to improve upon yourself as a leader—and as a human being.

MINDSET APPLIED

In Chapter 4, I talked about how the first three dimensions of IL all work together to form a foundational *mindset* of great leadership. Thinking differently, cultivating vulnerability, and embracing a duty mindset work together to help us achieve the *perspective* we need in order to develop as leaders. As we move into the fourth dimension, we begin to make the shift into *applying* the perspective we've been cultivating to the concrete, nuts-and-bolts mechanics of great leadership.

This starts with leveraging your gifts and addressing your gaps, which is, in many ways, the crux of human development. It's where we identify the ways we need to improve, embrace the areas in which we already shine, and then put those all together to unlock our leadership potential.

Developing an accurate "map" of yourself, as we discussed above, is the first step in this process. But it is equally important that we use this information correctly. For example, as we'll explore later, many of the leaders I work with tend to undervalue their strengths—to take them for granted in such a way that they limit their own potential. The same goes for our "gaps." Many people tend to overreact to any negative feedback they receive because they don't see their flaws in the proper context. So as we move forward in the chapter, we'll create our maps by evaluating our gifts and gaps, and we'll also focus on how we *respond* to the information we're receiving from others and discuss how to best *apply* it to our lives and work.

Before we go any further, let's do a preliminary exercise. I want you to create two simple lists. The first should include your five biggest strengths or gifts as a human being and a leader. What are the qualities that you think others admire in you? What are the areas where you feel the most confident, and that you feel make the biggest contribution to those around you? Your second list should include the five areas where you think you could improve—qualities that, if developed, would make the biggest impact on your life. We'll return to these lists later in the chapter to get a sense of just how accurate your assessment was, and how you can best leverage your gifts and address your gaps moving forward.

THE NEGATIVITY BIAS

In the work that I do with leaders, we spend a good chunk of our time together assessing strengths and weaknesses (see the MLEI and Figure 1.2 on page 13). And I've noticed an interesting trend. People tend to be far more interested in their weaknesses and what they can improve upon than they are in what they already do well. Most people, it turns out, have a kind of unconscious preference for hearing what's bad about them over what's good about them. This is the case even among extremely confident people with a high self-concept. A common response I get when sharing any feedback is "Okay, great. I get that I'm good at _____. But tell me more about the things I'm not good at." It's as if the positive feedback bounces right off and they can't wait to hear the bad news.

Is this case for you? When you completed the exercise above, was it easier for you to find and relate to your weaknesses than to your strengths? Was your list of gifts shorter than your list of gaps? And do you find yourself far more interested in exploring the latter?

This bias toward the negative can be puzzling at first, but is quite natural. In fact, some researchers suggest that our preference for critical feedback might actually be a kind of evolutionary adaptation in the human species. In his book *Abundance: The Future Is Better Than You Think*, Dr. Peter Diamandis (chairman and founder of the XPrize) cites a wide range of evolutionary psychology research that explores what is known as the "negativity bias." The theory goes that the human brain evolved in an environment where those individuals who could seek out danger and anticipate harmful situations were better suited for survival. Imagine living on the African savannah where predators lurked around every corner and you had to literally fight for every meal. If you could anticipate the hyena attack, you'd be more likely to survive! That was the environment in which our brains developed, and even thousands of years later, we still have a bias toward seeing the potential harm around us. Except now it's not lions or drought we're afraid of; it's subtler fears like being fired, paying the bills, or not living up to our potential.

The Abundance Mindset

Dr. Peter Diamandis's book *Abundance* provides some very interesting insights into the negativity bias, but the main focus of the book—and what makes it so relevant to Intelligent Leadership—is what is possible when you overcome the bias and adopt a more fundamentally optimistic view of yourself and the world.

The world we live in today, while not completely devoid of danger, is far "safer" than the world in which our ancient ancestors evolved. Think about it. Many of us spend most of our lives in protected environments where our physical survival is not at risk—living in air-conditioned homes, transporting ourselves with vehicles, having access to advanced medicine, and eating any kind of food we have a hankering for, easily available just down the street at the supermarket. Even many marginalized populations have access to government support and amenities that the nomadic tribes of prehistory could never have dreamed.

> While our world isn't perfect (and there are very real prob-
> lems and dangers that we need to pay attention to), it is also
> overwhelmingly abundant compared to the past. And yet we
> don't act like it. We don't take advantage of the extraordinary
> gifts and opportunities that are all around us—and inside of
> us—because we are still so focused on problems. We're wired
> to think that way.
>
> But imagine if you could deeply internalize just how much
> abundance and opportunity is all around you? When you can
> identify just how irrational are many of the subtle fears and
> self-imposed limitations that you walk around with, you start
> to get in touch with what I like to call an "abundance mind-
> set." This perspective opens you up to a realm of possibilities
> and creative solutions that you just can't see when you're only
> focused on problems and what might go wrong.

In my experience, negativity bias is even stronger when we
engage in any kind of personal or professional development work.
It makes sense, right? When you're looking to improve, you want
to find the things that you need to improve upon. There's a natural
tendency to want to find out what's holding you back. Many people think of their strengths as things they've already mastered, and
so don't need to spend a lot of time working on them. They mistak-
enly think that if they can simply address their weaknesses—their
bottom line—then everything else will improve as a result.

While there is some truth to this, and while it is absolutely
crucial to zero in on your gaps and address them, you also need
to give as much *or more* attention to the areas in which you are
already strong. In my sessions with executives, I ask them, "Have
your gifts and strengths served you well so far in your life?" Their
answer, of course, is always "yes." And my follow-up question is:
"Then why can't we focus on making them stronger than they are
today?" These gifts, in my experience, can not only help you to
better address your gaps, but can carry you to heights that you
could never achieve by just improving your weaknesses. As the

old sports aphorism goes, sometimes the best defense is a good offense. The key to unlocking our development may lie in unearthing and accentuating what we already have within us, more than adding new capacities and skills.

For example, one of my clients—a COO at a Fortune 500 company—was having a difficult time motivating her team to deal with an organizational transition that she was tasked with spearheading. We'll call her Rose Marie. She was a shy person by nature, and had been given feedback for years about how motivating people wasn't her strength. Rose Marie was great with numbers and logistics, but had trouble bringing others on board with her ideas and galvanizing them into action.

In her mind, Rose Marie thought the key to being a good motivator was delivering inspiring speeches during meetings, but she was terrified of public speaking, even in small groups. So she worked on her verbal communication skills, rehearsing what she would say to her team in front of a mirror before morning meetings, and even signing up for a Toastmasters class. Although she did experience a nominal improvement, all that work didn't really get her the result she was hoping for.

When Rose Marie started working with me, the first thing I did was to dispel the notion that somehow she needed to become something she was not: a great speaker. At this point in her life, she just wasn't ever going to be a Tony Robbins type. But that didn't mean she couldn't become a great motivator. I asked her to think about what had made her successful thus far in her career, her greatest strengths. The first thing that came to mind was that Rose Marie had a natural gift for taking complex problems and distilling them into easy-to-understand models, and creating step-by-step plans for addressing them. This is what had led her to become such a successful COO.

We explored how she could leverage this gift to better motivate her team. It turns out that people actually respond quite positively to her ability to simplify complex situations. So she really leaned into it. She spent the entire weekend developing a beautiful map of the organizational transition plan. Another of her strengths was her ability to identify with the particular circumstances of each individual, so she made sure to include the key roles and responsibilities of each team member.

When it came time to meet on Monday morning, Rose Marie unveiled her plan to the team and walked them through it step by step. Everyone was blown away. The clarity she brought to the situation—and the care that she gave to helping each team member to understand their particular role—turned out to be a great motivator for everyone involved. And she didn't even have to give a dreaded motivational speech.

In the example above, we identified one of Rose Marie's "signature strengths," as my colleague and fellow executive coach Avra Lyraki calls them. These are the innate abilities that each of us possess that have made us who we are today. They are usually responsible for the majority of the successes we've experienced in our lives, and yet they are so "us" that we often don't even acknowledge their existence or value. But buried within each of these signature strengths—underneath our deeply ingrained bias toward what's wrong with us—is an untapped potential.

The key is to identify these signature strengths, and then—like my client—lean into them and see how far they can take us. The best leaders, the truly great ones, are able to do this, and you can too. If you can overcome your negativity bias for just a moment and allow yourself to be even *more* of who you are, to add more weight to the extraordinary parts of yourself, I promise you'll be surprised—and pleased—by the results.

Now that we've explored the importance of leveraging your strengths, I'd like you to return to the list you made earlier. Are there innate strengths you'd like to add that you may have overlooked? Can you envision ways to better leverage your strengths in the future?

MIND THE GAP

Now that you've thoroughly explored your strengths, you should be in the right mindset to take a look at your weaknesses. Your gaps, as I like to call them, are simply the areas where you could really use some improvement. They could be skills that are under-developed, like strategic thinking, communication, or attention to detail. Or they might be character flaws, like having a hot temper or being too self-obsessed. Your gaps may be obvious to you— the kind of things you've gotten feedback about for years. Or they might be more subtle—issues that you need some help to unearth.

The key to identifying your gaps is seeking out the "limiting factors to growth." We're not looking to identify issues just for the sake of understanding yourself better (though that is a noble pursuit). We are shooting for results. We're all busy people, and we don't have time to improve on every single element of ourselves. I have a weakness for ice cream, but working on that is not likely to help me to be a better human being or be better at my job. So we want to find the areas that would have a significantly positive effect on everything else in our lives if we were to improve in them. These are the issues that, when combined with leveraging your gifts, will have the biggest impact on unleashing your potential.

My colleague Paul Cortissoz, founder of HR Soul Consulting, shared with me an example from his work of how zeroing in on a key weakness unleashed significant growth in one of his executive clients, Jason, the CMO of a big company. Like Rose Marie in the example above, Jason was having trouble motivating his team. Unlike Rose Marie, Jason was a brilliant visionary and had a penchant for getting his team fired up in meetings. But for some reason, the energy that he was able to inspire in meetings wasn't translating into real results. His team was chronically underperforming, in spite of having a lot of talent, and he was beginning to get frustrated.

As is common with many visionary types, Jason was having a hard time seeing his own responsibility in his team's performance issues. He was a very competent individual, and he felt like he was doing everything he could to fire people up. They were just falling short. Paul persisted, and was able to get Jason into a vulnerable enough state that he could start to consider the possibility that there might be something about his leadership style that was contributing to his team's lack of follow-through.

It turns out that Jason was a classic "big picture guy" and that he had a real aversion to getting into the details. By being vulnerable, Jason was able to solicit honest feedback from his team members, and they painted a picture of an environment where they felt inspired, but also somewhat abandoned by him. Jason would get things moving and then leave the details to everyone else. He didn't make the effort to at least familiarize himself with the more logistical side of their work and listen to the issues his team was facing. This meant that Jason's "big picture" thinking wasn't informed by the very concrete implications of putting that vision into practice. It also meant that his team didn't feel any sense of empathy from him, and that hampered their desire to perform for him, no matter how inspiring his talks could be.

So, with Paul's help, Jason began taking a much bigger interest in the day-to-day operations of his team. He established daily check-ins with all the key stakeholders, making the effort to appreciate the specifics they were dealing with in each of their roles. He didn't abandon his big picture thinking—that was one of his greatest gifts—but added a much-needed element of embracing the practical implications of those ideas.

Jason's newfound attention to detail didn't become a signature strength, but it was no longer something that was holding him back. Even more, it actually accentuated his other strengths. Embracing the practical implications of his "big picture thinking" made it stronger, more rooted in reality. As a result, Jason's inspirational talks stopped falling on the deaf ears of his team members. They trusted him more, because they could see that he was making the effort to take their particular circumstances into consideration.

GOING ON TO PERFECTION

Facing your own flaws can be one of the most difficult aspects of the leadership development process. It's hard to admit your imperfections, and it's even harder to start to address them. One of the biggest reasons for this has to do with the mindset that we bring to the self-assessment process. And I believe that if we want to be able to respond to our "gaps" in the most constructive way possible, we need to cultivate a more fluid perspective on ourselves and our imperfections.

Most of us tend to view ourselves as static entities, with our flaws as symptoms of how we are falling short of some idea of perfection that we've had our whole lives. But the truth is, we are much more dynamic than we tend to think, and our flaws are a natural part of our growth as human beings. There's a phrase from John Wesley, an eighteenth-century British theologian, that I've always found compelling. He describes the human journey as one of "going on to perfection." In other words, no one is perfect, but we can always be striving for perfection.

I believe that all of us—no matter how flawed or extraordinary—are works in progress. There is always room to improve, and therefore there are always "gaps" to address. From this perspective, a weakness isn't so much a "flaw" or a mistake. It's an opportunity for growth. It's the next challenge we can take on to move ourselves closer to perfection.

Believe it or not, viewing ourselves as a work in progress is connected back to the duty mindset that we explored in Chapter 4. Remember, the "duty mindset" we are striving for is essentially remaining in touch with the truth of how deeply interconnected we are to the matrix of relationships that make up our lives. When we make the effort to improve upon an element of ourselves, like Jason did in the example above, it has ripple effects on those around us. We start to see ourselves not so much as static individuals who are "falling short" of perfection, but as facilitators of growth. Our gaps, then, are not just our own. They are gaps in the entire complex system that we belong within, and are opportunities for us to improve the lives of everyone around us.

Now that we've explored the concept of "gaps" more deeply, let's take a moment to reflect. What would you say are highest-leverage areas of improvement for you? What are the weaknesses that you feel are holding back most of your energy and inhibiting improvement? This is a good time to reach out to your trusted peer network. Are they bringing new issues to the table that maybe you weren't aware of?

Remember, as you begin the process of addressing your gaps, I suggest that you strive to be an *"on to* perfectionist." Avoid perfectionism! Cultivate a mindset of constantly striving for improvement, while not being disappointed, shocked, or intimidated by the fact that you are full of flaws. That's the only healthy way to address your gaps, and the only way you'll be able to truly improve upon them.

STRIKING THE RIGHT BALANCE

Remember the analogy of the map from the beginning of this chapter? As you create the map of your inner territory—your strengths and your weaknesses—it is imperative that you strike the right balance. I want to reiterate just how important it is that as you begin to assess your gaps, be very light with yourself. Don't get too bogged down on any one thing, and try to keep your emotions out of it. Approach your gaps as a scientist would: objectively and analytically. Think of your personality as something to be studied and improved upon. In short, don't take it personally. However, on the flip side, avoid getting carried away with exploring your strengths. It is very easy to overlook some of the "downsides" that come with both our strengths and our weaknesses.

For example, say you're discovering that you have a talent for strategic thinking that you haven't been leveraging. You can often see the "forest" when others are focused on the trees, and start to be more assertive in the big-picture thinking that comes naturally to you. That's great! But in the process, you don't want to get a big head about it. You don't want to now overlook the importance of a more detail-oriented perspective and become overconfident in your own view. You also don't want to mistake any of the progress or success that you experience from leveraging your strengths to make you think that you have somehow "arrived" or achieved some kind of perfection. Even LeBron James, arguably the best basketball player on earth, works on new skills every year. There is always further to go.

No matter how great you are, there's always room to improve. And even if you are a deeply flawed individual, there are untapped potentials that you may not be seeing.

ZEROING IN, MOVING FORWARD

When you truly master the art of leveraging your gifts and addressing your gaps, you will develop a natural preference for having the clearest picture possible of yourself at all times. You'll always want to be gathering as much feedback as you can so you can be sure you know what you need to improve on—because you'll continually want to be changing and developing. Having that goal will enable you to handle all feedback with maturity and to take action to address what you find without overreacting.

Keep in mind that even the most mature leader will sometimes have difficulty naturally embodying this dimension. From time to time, she will need to manually get herself into the right mindset to seek and respond to feedback. All of us need work in this dimension, and there are very concrete things that we can do to start the process of self-assessment. Below are a series of exercises and behaviors that you can use to put this dimension into practice.

A 360-Degree View

The first step in the process of mastering this dimension of Intelligent Leadership is to get what I call a "360-degree view" of yourself. This step involves assessing both your strengths and your weaknesses. It also includes seeing both gross and subtle aspects of your behavior or character—a combination of obvious characteristics, like your communication habits, and harder-to-see elements, like how you perceive yourself as a leader. When I help clients to develop their own 360-view, we use a combination of self-assessments (with tools like the MLEI; visit johnmattone.com/booktools for free access) and outreach to their peer network. This way we get a full-spectrum view of each person, using subjective and objective feedback. You can use these tools, too, to help you develop your own 360-degree view of yourself.

I use a medical analogy to reinforce to leaders how vital it is to be extraordinarily accurate about what our strengths and gaps are. In medicine, there is a common adage that "prescription before diagnosis is malpractice." Any doctor who prescribes medicine without having utilized multiple diagnostics to determine an accurate and clear diagnosis will prescribe the wrong medicine, the wrong dosage, and the wrong care plan. Think of the ramifications in such a scenario. There is no room in medicine for any doctor not to have completed a thorough diagnostic. The same is true in the world of leadership and personal development. In order to create an effective plan for improvement, we need to have an accurate diagnosis!

This takes a lot of vulnerability, especially at first. You have to be willing to be brutally honest with yourself. And you have to humble yourself enough to ask the key stakeholders in your life to share their unvarnished perspective. But what almost everyone finds when they engage in this process is a profound increase in trust, confidence, and clarity. I suggest that you take some time at this point in the process to do your own 360-degree assessment. Make a list of both your strengths and your weaknesses, then reach out to your peer network to get their feedback.

Ask for Go-Forward Suggestions (GFS)

As you review your 360 results and any other feedback you have received in the past, it's important to recognize that *whatever happened in the past—happened in the past.* It cannot be changed, and there's no value in dwelling on old mistakes. One way to help keep your mindset more future-oriented is to reframe the way you go about seeking feedback. Instead of asking others to simply tell you about things they think you do or don't do well, consider asking them for what I call "go-forward suggestions" (GFS). For example: "Mary Lou, what are some go-forward suggestions you have for me to consider in order to improve how I communicate?" The GFS approach is powerful because it will implicitly address your past mistakes and flaws, but do so in a way that doesn't make you defensive or regretful. A GFS focuses on solutions and potential, which is what Intelligent Leadership is all about. We don't want to know ourselves simply for the sake of having more self-knowledge. We want to improve and become better leaders and better human beings. Seeking GFS keeps you and those you seek feedback from aligned with this results-oriented mentality.

Make a Plan, Keep It Simple

Once you've gotten a clear sense of your gifts and gaps, it's time to make a plan for how to address them. For your gifts, you want to focus on how each one could be given greater focus in your life. For your gaps, you should look for ways to improve upon weaknesses and curtail the negative consequences of behaviors that aren't serving you. Remember, it's not possible to become a new person. Your gaps will always be there. But you can become aware of them and develop strategies for making sure that they don't wreak havoc on yourself or those around you.

As you develop your action plan, make sure to keep it simple. You want one or two strategies for each quality you're tackling. Keep those strategies concise. For example: I will improve my ability to lead constructive team meetings by a) spending at least an hour preparing for each meeting, and b) getting more input from stakeholders beforehand. Make sure that you include target dates for each, and share your plan with someone you trust who can hold you accountable.

Finally, don't bite off more than you can chew. You should never be working on more than two strengths and two development needs or gaps at a time. Start small and then build on your successes by adding new elements to your plan. It's better to succeed initially with a lighter plan than to fail with a more ambitious one.

Become an Expert in Yourself

The end goal of this process is for you to become the world's foremost expert on yourself. You want to know, more than anyone else, the ins and outs of your strengths and weaknesses. If others know you better than you know yourself, you're bound to cause problems. You'll be like a bull in a china shop, and you probably won't even know it. But if you muster the courage and vulnerability to study yourself, using the feedback of others, you'll know your own shadow and you'll perceive your impact on the world, both positive and negative. This self-knowledge is priceless.

CHAPTER **6**

Having the Courage to Execute with Pride, Passion, and Precision

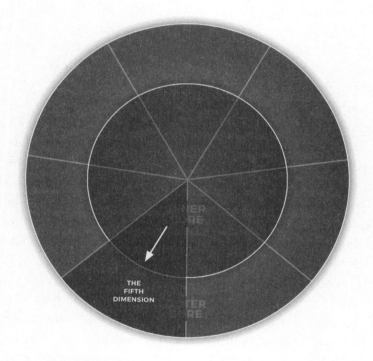

My eldest son Nick's passion growing up was basketball. And he was good. Really good. Thanks to a combination of natural talent and an intense work ethic, he became one of the top high school basketball players in the country, received a scholarship to play Division I college basketball, and eventually played professionally in Europe before an injury prematurely ended his career.

One of the things that I have always admired about Nick—and one of the qualities that made him so successful with his game—was his willingness to "show up" in the biggest moments, every time. He was clutch. He knew that when the ball was tipped and the game began, nothing else mattered except what was happening right there on the court. All the practice, all the past victories and failures, all the preparation in the world didn't matter once the game started. At game time, he had to shift into a new gear and perform. No excuses. He knew that he had to execute.

As we begin our exploration of the fifth dimension of Intelligent Leadership, we are entering our own version of "game time." This is the point in our journey where the rubber meets the road. It's with this dimension, "Having the Courage to Execute with Pride, Passion, and Precision," that we make a fundamental shift from perspective to action. Much of the work we did in the first four dimensions primarily developed self-awareness. Now, with the fifth dimension, our work starts to translate this perspective into action.

Nick's ability to execute when it mattered most is what separated him from other players who may have had as much or more talent than he did. It's also what separates the truly great leaders from the rest of the pack. The willingness to act under pressure is a key quality that separates the pretenders from the real difference-makers. Great leaders know that all the brilliance or talent in the world means nothing if you can't turn it into action. They understand implicitly that thorough analysis, planning, and preparation are each crucial for success, but are useless if they don't ultimately translate into results. They know that, in the words of Master Yoda from Star Wars, "Do, or do not. There is no try."

MOVING OUT OF YOUR COMFORT ZONE

While the ability to execute might seem pretty straightforward, it's actually quite rare. As I write these pages, it's January, the beginning of the year: resolutions season. New Year's resolutions, and their short shelf-life, are a perfect example of just how rare, and difficult, execution can be. Resolutions provide endless comedic fodder, because they tend to be so boldly proclaimed each January, and yet so predictably abandoned by the end of Q1. Just because we *plan* to do something doesn't mean that we *will*. Executing requires courage. You need steel nerves to take a vision and actualize it, whether that vision is a project plan, a New Year's resolution, or a book.

Why? When reality sets in, turning our plans and goals into action is usually much more difficult than we expect it will be. When you're in the position of acting on a plan or vision—no matter how big or small the job—you will inevitably step out of your comfort zone into new, unfamiliar territory. There are obstacles and curve balls you could never anticipate. And there are countless internal and external forces that always seem to wait until game time to appear.

Many people find this too much. They'd rather let someone else lead the way. They hesitate to take responsibility for making things happen. This is fine, of course, but it isn't leadership. Truly great leaders are those who are willing to lean into the often uncomfortable position of executing a plan. They are the ones who have the courage to step into the unknown on behalf of everyone involved.

CULTIVATING COURAGE, IN SPITE OF RESISTANCE

If this dimension makes you feel a little nervous, that's a good thing. The demand for results—the pressure to execute—creates a natural resistance in even the most courageous individual. It pushes against the part of us that would rather take the comfortable route and avoid the accountability of delivering. That's the thing: We all feel the resistance to execute, but the leaders among us are the ones who cultivate an ability to act in spite of that resistance.

Cultivating this courage is something anyone can do. Courage, as you may remember from Chapter 1 in our discussion of character, is being willing to take action in the face of adversity or pressure. This is something you can start doing immediately, and you can start small.

My colleague, Lyne Cathcart, has a unique approach to helping her clients cultivate courage in their lives. Whenever they do something she feels exhibits even a small degree of courage, she gives them the "Golden Balls Award." While humorous, her award is intended to validate the action her client has taken, and to encourage her client's new internal momentum to grow and flourish into greater acts of courage and character.

Remember, being courageous doesn't necessarily look like the actions of a comic book superhero. As we have discussed, some of the most courageous acts are subtle: daring to be vulnerable, facing and admitting your flaws, doing something differently than you have done before. In fact, even though Lyne's Golden Balls Award sounds like something directly out of the John Wayne Leadership Playbook, she usually gives it to her clients when they've exhibited an act of "heroic vulnerability." The courage to execute can take many forms, as long as it's rooted in action.

THE THREE QUALITIES OF COURAGEOUS ACTION

So what does it look like to execute with courage? This, of course, depends on the individual and the circumstances. Anyone taking responsibility to translate vision into action exhibits a degree of this leadership dimension. But there are three qualities of courageous action that I've found to be universal: executing with pride, executing with passion, and executing with precision. Over the course of the chapter, we'll explore all three qualities, defining what they look like in the context of Intelligent Leadership, and how you can cultivate them yourself.

Let's start with executing with pride.

Taking Pride in What You Do

There are two sides to every coin. The same is true of pride. On one side, pride can take the form of stubbornness, egotism, or arrogance. This negative pride leads people to puff out their chests and hold the deluded idea that only they have the answers to pretty much everything. This expression of pride makes people overconfident in their abilities, alienates others, and ultimately gets in the way of their success.

On the other side of this coin is positive pride that, in the right proportions, is an important quality of leadership. It is directly tied to taking action, and is based on "taking pride" in what you do. For example, I have a friend who is a very talented woodworker. He makes the most beautiful tables and cabinetry, and he is uncompromising in his craft. He takes great pride in his work, and not in an arrogant way. He feels an obligation to the quality of the craft itself, and he holds himself—and anyone working with him—to a high standard. This results in a quiet confidence in his work that is remarkable.

The same is true of leadership. If you take pride in what you do, and hold yourself to a high standard of excellence, you'll exude natural leadership. Positive pride is earned, and can't be faked or mimicked because it is the result of committing to something from start to finish and holding yourself accountable for delivering results. Positive pride accumulates—with each successful outcome, you gain confidence in your ability to act. This has a cumulative effect, so with each future action, you'll be able to draw on the pride you've earned. This is pride with weight, pride that people respect, and pride that you yourself can count on to get you through difficult times.

Think of how you've felt after following through on something difficult, versus when you've given up prematurely. A simple example, for me, is my daily workout. When I wake up every morning, the last thing I want to do is hit the gym. I'm tired, anxious about everything I have to accomplish in the day ahead, and full of reasons why I don't need to make the effort to keep my body in shape. When I ignore all those voices in my head and go forward with the workout, I always feel better—and not just physically. I feel proud. I feel stronger and more confident in my own ability to overcome whatever resistance I may be facing, internally and externally.

Again, wholesome pride can't be faked. This is both bad news and good news. The bad news is that if you want to bring pride to your actions, you have to do the work. There are no shortcuts! Fake pride is arrogance, and people sense it a mile away. The good news is that positive pride is something that any one of us can start to earn right away. It comes from taking action, even when it's not convenient or comfortable, and holding yourself to a standard of excellence. Every time you execute with earned pride, you reinforce the best part of yourself.

Where's the Passion?

We've all had the experience of being so passionate about something that everything else seems to fade into the background: Perhaps you experience passion while you're leading the way on a big campaign at work or maybe when you're coaching your child's soccer team or doing home improvement projects, or playing music or painting. Whatever the activity, you are so enamored and engrossed that you give everything to it. Passion, I believe, is one of the key drivers of nearly all human endeavors, and I've found that activating your passion is an absolutely crucial element in strong leadership.

My passion is activated when I speak in front of a group—here, I'm in my element. The passion I have for public speaking makes me get out of bed in the morning, and has me traveling to the far ends of the earth. Because of that passion, I've been willing to tackle—and eventually overcome—the many obstacles that over the years have stood in the way of becoming a successful speaker. Today, I'm lucky enough to speak in front of large audiences at conferences and at company events. But it took me a long time to get to this point. I spent years traveling around the country from small gig to small gig, briefcase in hand, staying in dingy motels. I didn't make good money, and I had to spend way too much time away from my family. But I persisted, in part, because I was so passionate about it. And eventually it paid off.

Passion, it turns out, is one of our greatest allies in finding the wherewithal to take action in the face of resistance. We need it in order to execute courageously. And yet it's not always available to us. Sometimes we lose access to passion, and a particular activity, or career path, or even life in general, just starts to feel dull. In those moments, passion doesn't flow naturally; it needs to be manually applied. But how?

In my experience, the most powerful way to ignite your passion is to connect with your core purpose. Your core purpose, you may remember from the first dimension of Intelligent Leadership, is a kind of thesis statement for your life—it's the big vision for who you are and why you are here on this earth. I like to spend some time every day to think about my core purpose. When life is flowing, this is a kind of affirming experience. But in moments when it seems as if the passion has gone away, taking the time to get in touch with this fundamental orientation can serve as a kind of a North Star to guide you through the wilderness. Ultimately, you want your connection to that purpose to be so powerful and deeply clear that it can survive the inevitable ups and downs of life and be a constant source of strength.

By cultivating your deeper passion, the one connected to your core purpose, you'll more easily close the gap between vision and action. You'll be able to keep moving forward, with energy, even when it seems like everything and everyone is against you.

Executing with Precision

There are certain areas of life that require more precision than others. If you're flying a plane or performing heart surgery, for example, your attention to detail—or lack thereof—has bigger consequences than if you're mowing the lawn or tossing a football with friends. In leadership, it is the "game time" situations that demand more of your attention and focus. The best leaders have the ability to perceive when and where more precision is required, and have the mettle to execute with appropriate precision in those moments.

The benefits of acting with precision are obvious. You make fewer mistakes, leave less to chance, and ultimately run a tighter ship. You're much less likely to be successful if you're sloppy. But there's another benefit to precision that you may not have considered, which has more to do with mindset. When you hold yourself to a standard of precision, it creates an intense focus on the success of whatever you're engaged in, and that mindset affects your entire team. Suddenly, you and your team are not just going through the motions, but you're each bringing a much higher level of awareness to the task at hand. I call it a "laser focus," because like a focused beam of light, this awareness has the power to penetrate nearly any challenge or obstacle you're presented with.

Acting with precision also helps you to better leverage your time and energy. When your team is laser-focused on an outcome, you're all less likely to get sidetracked, and your actions will all be moving toward the same goal. It's easier to set priorities and avoid anything that doesn't contribute to the prime directive of what you're working on. Being laser-focused creates momentum that builds on itself. And this momentum is contagious. As a leader, you're responsible for setting the tone for others. When you're bringing a high degree of precision and focus, it inspires the same in others. It keeps people on track, holds them to a higher standard, and elevates them into the same laser-focused mindset that you're bringing on a day-to-day basis.

The Power of Three

When you commit yourself to a high degree of precision and focus, everything you do becomes supercharged. You stop wasting time or making silly mistakes, and you begin to generate momentum that compels people around you. You're taking great pride in what you're doing, you're passionate in how you execute, and you're holding yourself and others to a standard of precision. It's a winning combination. When you learn to execute with these qualities, the natural result is the kind of courageous action that all great leaders know how to take when it matters most. When it's game time.

CHANGE TAKES COURAGE

The most effective leaders are those who have built a habit of taking action, because it is they who are the most prepared to move with confidence in the face of change. As a leader, you must be prepared to deal with the constant reality of change, whether it is in developing your leadership capacities, or trying to change the systems and culture within a company. And the thing is, change is hard. This is why you need to master what I call the art of courageous action.

By definition, change requires you to step outside your comfort zone into new and unknown territory. When you're trying to change your own behavior, you may often feel as if you're in one of those bad dreams where you show up at school with no clothes on—completely unprepared and caught off-balance. When you're trying to change an entire culture, you inevitably invite negativity and pushback from everyone around you. In these circumstances, you may find yourself vulnerable, and may find that you have little experience to help you figure out which way to go and what to do next. Many people simply freeze up when they find themselves outside their comfort zone, and they lose the ability to move forward.

This is when the courage to act becomes so important. If you've built a habit of courageous action—of acting with pride, passion, and precision—then you'll have more confidence to step into the unknown, even when you have no reference point. Mastering this dimension of Intelligent Leadership makes you more comfortable outside of your comfort zone. You're not intimidated by change. In fact, you embrace it.

Courage as Duty

This dimension of Intelligent Leadership can be very challenging for many people. Executing, especially with the courage we've been discussing, isn't easy, and takes guts. If you're finding it difficult to engage this dimension, you might try a trick that I often use with my clients: If you can't take action for yourself, do it for others. Just as we explored in the duty mindset chapter, we are all part of a vast network of relationships, and there are many people depending on us. I've found that thinking of yourself from this vantage point often inspires the courage to take even the most difficult action.

One of the more powerful experiences of how duty can inspire courage comes from the work I did with a client of mine. Alfredo is the CEO of the Mexico and South American division of a large multinational marketing firm. He was a good leader, and had hired me to help him bring his game to the next level. A big part of the work that I do with all of my clients is a 360-degree assessment. They take personalized assessments, and I also reach out to their employees, bosses, and team members to get their impressions. Once I've gotten all the feedback, we then work together to create a leadership development plan to leverage their gifts and address their gaps. The most important and final component of the process is when I ask the client to present both their assessment results and initial leadership development plan to their team.

Alfredo had a surprisingly easy time with all of the steps in the process—with the exception of the final presentation to his team. When it came time to share the results with his team, he got cold feet. We had called a meeting with eighteen members of his senior leadership team, and they had assembled themselves in the conference room, awaiting Alfredo's presentation. But he was terrified that admitting his flaws to his direct subordinates would make them respect him less. He literally froze, and couldn't find the courage to leave his office. So I broadened the context for him. I told him how important it was to everyone on his team that he do this. If he could find the courage to be vulnerable, he would inspire all of them. He would literally model for them what great leadership was through his own courageous action.

That did the trick. Inspired by this "other-oriented" motive, Alfredo found the courage to walk his team through the results of his assessment results and his leadership development plan. He bravely shared the areas where he needed to improve his own leadership and his plans for doing so. The result was nothing less than profound. He told his team members that he could only be as good a leader as they supported him in being, and that he needed each and every one of them. By the end of his presentation, his team members literally stood up and gave him a standing ovation. He was so overcome with gratitude for their support, that he embraced each one of them, with tears in his eyes.

Alfredo had a direct experience of how his obligation to others could give him the courage to do something that he had considered impossible. It empowered him as a leader and built a strong sense of trust within his core leadership team.

THE ULTIMATE CATALYST

I wasn't much of a science student growing up, but I have a lasting memory of one particular experiment that we conducted in my high school chemistry class. We poured one clear liquid into a beaker, and then slowly added another liquid into the container, drop by drop, watching for a change. For the first several drops, the color of the liquid in the beaker would remain clear. But then suddenly, one drop would cause all the liquid to instantaneously turn blue. The drops, at the right volume, served as a catalyst for transformation.

This dimension of Intelligent Leadership has a similar catalytic effect on each of the other dimensions. When you add courageous action to any one of them, it becomes supercharged, or amplified. Courageous action is the one element that brings all the others together, and takes us from big vision to transformative action.

Take for example the first dimension, "Thinking Differently, Thinking Big." As we discussed in that chapter, one of the potential weaknesses of big thinking is that it remains just that: big thinking. We've all met our fair share of "idea guys" who love to talk a big game, but even their most brilliant ideas don't lead to much real change. It takes courage to act on big thinking. As you cultivate this dimension of Intelligent Leadership, you develop an ability to bring even the loftiest ideas into reality. Your ideas are rooted in the realities of implementation, and therefore carry much more weight. Intelligent leaders know how to think *and* act big.

When it comes to the second dimension, the vulnerability decision, courage is absolutely crucial. Unlike what the John Waynes of the world might suggest, being vulnerable is one of the most courageous acts you can make as a leader. Vulnerability is not the kind of thing that you can think yourself into. You have to act, in spite of any fears or discomfort you might have. Again, action is a key catalyst for being vulnerable.

In the "Courage as Duty" sidebar earlier in the chapter, I talked about the power that the duty mindset has on helping you find the courage to act in difficult situations. Remember, this mindset is based on a recognition of how many people are depending on you. When you take action in this context, it has ripple effects far beyond yourself.

Finally, and perhaps most significantly, action is a crucial ingredient in leveraging your gifts and addressing your gaps. While self-knowledge is important, and there are significant benefits that come simply from understanding your strengths and your weaknesses, the real power of this dimension comes when you actually change your behavior based on that understanding. One of the reasons that this dimension is so powerful is that many of us have strengths that we don't act upon nearly enough. And when we are faced with our gaps, we don't have the courage to rise up and address them, to do the necessary work to improve upon the areas that hold us back. Action is the secret sauce that makes all of this work.

DON'T JUST ACT; ACT INTELLIGENTLY

When understood correctly, this dimension of Intelligent Leadership has nothing but benefits. However, there are some common pitfalls that people find when they're trying to take on the challenge of executing with pride, passion, and precision. The biggest danger is a tendency to focus too exclusively on action, and lose the broader context in which action is being taken. If you're a "doer," or someone who feels uncomfortable taking their time or moving cautiously, then this might be something that you should look out for in particular.

I find this happens to me sometimes during very busy periods of work. I'll wake up in the morning, open up my inbox, and just start responding. I have so much work to do that I feel like I just need to attack it all with pure action. But this often leads to me using my time inefficiently, getting burned out, or losing sight of my bigger priorities. I act blindly, and it leads to problems.

This same tendency can happen at much more significant levels. When you're facing a large and complex problem, either personally or professionally, there can be a strong temptation just to react. And this often happens without a lot of thought. I recently had a client who was facing a situation like this say to me that instead of simply being "reactive," he was striving to be "strategic." He was taking the necessary time to think through the situation from multiple angles, before moving into execution.

This is an essential quality of leadership. You, as a leader, need to have an ability to distinguish between the times when action is necessary and the times when more strategy is needed. You can either inspire your team into action, or hold action back for the sake of thinking things through more thoroughly. The best leaders act intelligently.

So while you cultivate the courage to act, it's important that you also keep a big view on yourself and what you're doing. Don't mistake strategic thinking for the kind of "overthinking" that often gets in the way of courageous action. While you never want to avoid taking action, it's crucial that you take the time to understand why you're doing things and how they fit into the bigger strategies and visions that drive you on a day-to-day basis. Courageous action also needs to be intelligent action.

BECOMING COURAGEOUS

You may think that some people are born with naturally high capacity for taking courageous action, and that you're not one of those people. However, in my experience, this dimension of Intelligent Leadership requires a lot of practice, and effort. Taking action in the face of obstacles and resistance—both internal and external—is challenging. Period. And honestly, most of us aren't wired to take fearless, courageous action. We tend to avoid challenging situations and do our best to stay within our comfort zones. But if you want to be a leader—a truly courageous one—then it's imperative that you develop your courage muscles. You need to build a habit of running toward obstacles rather than away from them.

Following are a series of igniter behaviors that you can take to develop, or accentuate, your own capacity for courageous action. They aren't so much a "how-to" guide as they are the building blocks of courageous action. They are both exercises and qualities.

(Re)Connect with Your Core Purpose

In Chapter 2, we set the course for our Intelligent Leadership journey by creating a core purpose statement (CPS). As you may recall, your CPS is the biggest possible vision you can create for your life and work. It is based on deep questions, like "Why am I here?" and "What have I been put on this earth to do?" In contrast, this chapter has been all about action, and finding the courage to execute with pride, passion, and precision. In my experience, the deepest possible source of courage comes from having a strong and well-considered vision for yourself—one that is big enough to keep you afloat in the rough seas of life.

When the executives I work with believe in and embrace the power of doing this deeper work *first*, they not only take positive action in response, but do so with incredible pride, passion, and precision. By tapping into the depths of your soul—perhaps for the first time—and creating the vision of the essence of the person and leader you must become, you start to see that your own journey is actually *less* about you and much *more* about others. You start to realize that your own pursuit of happiness and centeredness is not a selfish pursuit at all, as you now see that your own happiness is fueled by the happiness you bring to others. This "other-oriented" motivation generates a tremendous amount of courage.

So at this point in the process, I suggest that you take some time to reconnect with your core purpose statement. If you skipped over that exercise, no problem! This is a great excuse to go back and do it. As you get in contact with the big vision that your CPS is based on, notice how it makes you feel. Do you feel you have more confidence to take action, regardless of what you're up against? The answer, for most people, is a resounding yes.

Assessing and Taking Pride

As we've discussed at length in this chapter, having a healthy sense of pride in your work is a crucial part of courageous action. Wanting to be proud of yourself and your work is a mentality that you carry forward with you as you engage in any activity. Looking back on your past actions, the degree of pride you feel in your accomplishments is a measure of what kind of leader you've been up until now.

There's an exercise I do with many of my clients that I'd like to share with you. Think about the major actions you've taken over the past week, month, and year. These could be personal actions, like tackling a new workout regime or diet, or activities related to your work, like heading up an initiative. Make a list of two or three actions for each timescale (week/month/year). Now go through your actions and reflect on how proud you are of the work you did for each. Did you feel that what you did reflected your best effort?

Or did you cut corners just to get it done? Rate each action on a scale of one to ten, with ten being the highest degree of pride.

Once you've gone through your list, review your scores and reflect. Are these the measurements of someone who takes great pride in their work? Or do you have room to grow? For the actions with the highest scores, what about your work gave you the greatest sense of pride? Was it the quality of the work? Was it the fact that you persevered through something very challenging? Are you proud of the effect that your actions had on others? Now, identify the activities where you scored lower than the others, and reflect on why you're not as proud of what you did. What can you do to improve your approach to similar activities in the future?

This exercise, in and of itself, puts you in the mindset of someone who takes great pride in what they do, regardless of how proud you are of your past actions. This mindset is a foundation from which you can take new actions with a much greater sense of pride.

Finding and Unleashing Your Passion

Do you consider yourself to be a passionate person? Why or why not? Remember, I'm not talking about cliché definitions of what it means to be passionate (like loving Latin dance or being a connoisseur of fine wine and poetry). I'm talking about being so committed to something that you lose yourself in it. Passion is giving maximum effort toward something, not because you *have* to do it, but because you *want* to do it. Passion is the engine that drives courageous action.

Strangely, from what I've encountered thus far in my career as an executive coach as well as in my life outside of work, very few people consider themselves to be passionate. This is partially because we aren't familiar with the broadest sense of the word, and partially because we just can't see it in ourselves. For this reason, reaching out to others—your peer network—is a great way to get a sense of just how passionate you are and where your passions lie. You can talk to your loved ones, peers, or trusted friends. Ask them how "passionate" they consider you to be. Ask for specifics as well, such as: In what areas of life are you most passionate? What are some examples where they've witnessed your passion?

Once you've gotten a good set of answers, review them. Do the responses surprise you? Do your peers see passion that you are not aware of? Are there things you are passionate about that no one mentioned? Most people find that this exercise gives them a new window into themselves. More importantly, it connects them with a deeper sense of passion—not a passion for specific things, but a more universal passion that provides fuel for all their actions.

CHAPTER **7**

Staying Present and Being Vigilant

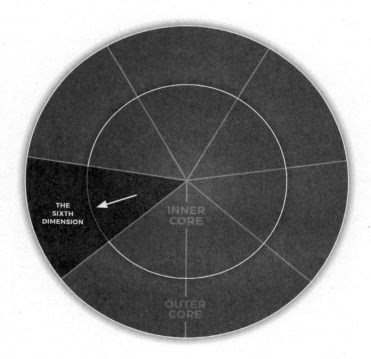

It's not exactly a profound cultural insight to suggest that we live in the Age of Distraction. Simply look around in any public space—on a train, in a coffee shop, or even on the sidewalk—and you're likely to see the majority of people "plugged in," headphones on and eyes glued to their phone or tablet. Smartphones and almost unlimited access to the internet, along with the emergence of multiple social media platforms, have created a world in which most of us are constantly bombarded with information. A 2018 study by Udemy Research[1] found that three out of every four workers feel distracted at work, and a surprising 36 percent of millennial and Gen Z workers spend at least two hours per day on their phones for nonwork activities. Indeed, it often feels as if we are drowning in a continuous stream of text message alerts, Instagram updates, and phone calls, all of which carry a high demand for our attention.

Attention, it seems, is at a premium.

Meanwhile, the pace of life and work seem to be speeding up as well. Our new technological reality allows us to cram much more into each day—activities, projects, relationships, and even jobs. We can now be in multiple places at the same time, albeit virtually. A friend recently told me that he took a ski weekend, and conducted business calls from his cell phone on the chairlift. Thanks to all of these opportunities for adding more to our lives, we're more productive than ever. However, we are also experiencing a greater and greater demand on our time. At work, and even in our personal lives, we are under increased pressure to move quickly, often at the expense of taking the sufficient amount of time to make good decisions and get things right. Not only that, but finding space in our schedules for our minds to relax or reflect is becoming a job in itself.

This time pressure is particularly strong for leaders and managers. The demand to perform and deliver, and to do it quickly, becomes more intense as you move closer to the "top of the food chain." As a result, many leaders find that they often feel forced to cut corners and move faster than they'd like to. There is a growing sense of panic within individuals and organizations that gets in the way of good, solid, and often time-consuming strategic thinking.

---

[1] https://research.udemy.com/research_report/udemy-depth-2018-workplace-distraction-report/.

In this atmosphere of increased time pressure and information overload, there is a significant premium on leaders who are able to tune out the distractions and stay focused. I call this capacity "staying present and being vigilant." It is the sixth and perhaps most relevant dimension of Intelligent Leadership. Staying present allows you to be awake to the multidimensional complexity of the situations you're involved in. Being present in your interactions and relationships with others builds trust and improves communications. The more vigilant you are, the fewer mistakes you'll make, and the more effective and efficient you'll become.

I have found that today's great leaders are separated from the merely competent ones by their disciplined dedication to being present, no matter what kind of outside pressures they encounter. Yet it may be the most difficult element of Intelligent Leadership to put into practice, especially these days. It takes courage. It takes commitment. And most of all, the ability to rise above the distraction and be a truly present leader takes a profound dedication to improving the lives of those around you. Over the course of this chapter, we'll explore how.

MOVING SLOW TO MOVE FAST

One of the most important elements of being present and staying vigilant is taking the time to slow down and absorb each situation, decision, or moment, so that you can make more effective decisions. I have a friend, a former Navy officer, who has a favorite motto: "Slow is smooth and smooth is fast." The phrase, one she borrowed from the Navy SEALs, is based on the Latin *festina lente*, which translates as "hurry slowly." To her, the value in "hurrying slowly" is that when you're taking your time, you don't make mistakes. And when you don't make mistakes, you actually move faster. Alternatively, when you're rushing, you often end up acting with incomplete information and are much more prone to errors. And the amount of time it takes to clean up your mistakes ends up being far greater than the time you saved by rushing.

Moving slow in order to move fast, to many of us, seems like common sense. When we were children, we learned from the classic tale of "The Tortoise and the Hare" that sometimes it's better to move at a slower pace in order to "win the race." But we all know that putting that lesson into practice actually can be quite difficult, especially in high-pressure situations. In fact, it turns out that we are neurologically wired to move quickly.

In his 2011 best-selling book, *Thinking Fast and Slow*, behavioral psychologist and Nobel Prize–winning economist Daniel Kahneman lays out a thoughtful and well-researched argument for why "thinking slow" is so important in today's world. He identifies two different "systems" of thinking that we employ in any given situation. System 1 is intuitive—gut-thinking—based on our initial impressions. System 2 thinking is analytical, based on careful reflection and problem solving. To be more effective thinkers, we need to prioritize our analytical System 2 thinking, and deemphasize our intuitive System 1 thinking.

Certainly, this can be challenging, especially in our hyperdrive world. When we are moving fast, our natural tendency is to go with our guts (System 1 thinking). Mix into that what Kahneman says about our brains: They are wired to find patterns and create stories out of the information we are given, which helps us make sense of reality. But this pattern-finding capacity can backfire, especially when we are moving too fast, because we often find connections and narratives that are inaccurate and based on incomplete information. So in order to avoid making the mistake of going with our guts, or acting on incomplete information, we need to slow down, and take the time to use the right kind of thinking.

This is where being present comes in. When we are able to keep our attention focused and in the moment, we can start to understand the dynamics of our mind and be less susceptible to drawing premature conclusions. We can take the time necessary to use our System 2 thinking, and apply careful reflection and analysis to make choices and take actions that are based on more accurate information. In this way, we will become less prone to making mistakes and incorrect assumptions.

Time and time again, I've found this part of Intelligent Leadership to be difficult for my clients to grasp, at least initially. As we spend time exploring our values and thinking patterns, they are constantly asking me, "All of this analysis is great and all, John, but when do we get to the *action*?" My answer is always the same: We can't generate a prescription without first making the correct diagnosis. We need to take whatever time necessary to ensure we understand what's going on "under the hood" before we move into action. Failing to do so risks overlooking fundamental issues.

The best leaders are those who take the time to think things through, and encourage others to do the same, regardless of the time pressure they face. They understand that getting it done right is always more important than getting it done quickly, even if it means pushing back a deadline or not hitting a target. The best leaders are those who understand intimately the paradox of moving, and thinking, slowly in order to move fast.

Making the Space for Novelty

One powerful story about taking the time to stay present comes from Microsoft founder Bill Gates. Throughout his career as the head of one of the world's biggest technology companies, and even now as he runs the Bill and Melinda Gates Foundation, Mr. Gates has committed to carving out two weeks per year to fully unplug from his work, his family, and the world in general to think about the future. During these "Think Weeks," Gates isolates himself in a secret cabin in the woods, fully disconnected from internet, phone, TV, and news. He has no contact with his family, friends, or co-workers. The only thing he brings with him are books and proposals for new innovations. The goal of Gates's Think Weeks is to educate himself on the latest thinking in his field, and adjacent fields, and to think about the future.

These weeks in isolation work. He came up with the idea for the Microsoft tablet PC during a Think Week, and rumor has it that his 1995 retreat spurred him to write his famous memo "The Internet Tidal Wave." With the space to allow new ideas to flourish, he projected how the internet would soon transform the entire technology industry, and how Microsoft needed to change in order to avoid becoming obsolete.

Here you have one of the world's busiest humans finding the time—a full two weeks a year—simply to reflect on the current and future state of his industry. And he's not alone. I've encountered many examples of some of our greatest leaders, with more responsibility on their shoulders than most human beings, who somehow always seem to be able to find the time to step out of the day-to-day grind and find the space to expand their thinking.

BEING AWAKE TO YOUR FOOTPRINT

One of the ways that many of us have learned to survive in the age of information overload is to put our heads down, tune out the noise, and get to work. You block out the chaos of the world in order to stay focused and productive, tantamount to closing your door and hanging a "do not disturb" sign. While this almost maniacal focus may be beneficial in the short run, it cuts you off from the complex world of relationships and interactions around you. While you may be focused, you are "in your own head" and unaware of the consequences of your actions. True, we may feel efficient and focused when we act in this way, but more often than not, we end up wreaking havoc on those around us without even knowing it.

As appealing as it may be, tunnel vision just isn't acceptable if you want to be a leader. In Chapter 4, we discussed how leaders must act with a duty mindset—an awareness of the greater whole of which they are a part. You don't have the luxury of not being aware of your interconnectedness. It is true as well with the Intelligent Leadership dimension of staying present and being vigilant: You are keenly aware of your "behavioral footprint." You are striving to be vigilant, in part, so you can understand the impact you are having on those around us. When we are in touch with our footprint, we have a much better chance of making it a positive one! Our actions can lift people up, make work more efficient, or solve problems. If we ignore our impacts, we risk making already challenging situations even worse.

The greatest leaders are those who understand how much their actions, gross or subtle, actually affect those around them. I'll never forget something that one of my clients, Henry, told me on this point. Henry was the CFO for a midwestern energy company. He was an old-school exec, the brand of man who always left the house clean shaven and appropriately dressed. He told me, "John, for me, first impressions are renewed every day. Every morning on my way to work, I think about everyone on my team and how I might be able to brighten up their day. That practice helps me enter the office with energy, no matter what else might be going on in my life. I can 'show up' for everyone else and show them, through my own example, that today's outlook is good."

Henry really understood the effect he had on others, and he had his own way of making sure he never forgot it. Even something as subtle as whether he was smiling when he walked into his office every morning was important to him—and to those around him, even if they weren't necessarily aware of it. This is the power of being present. You can see even the smallest ripples that emanate from what you do and how you are. Your influence won't always be perfectly positive, but if you make the effort to keep your behavioral footprint in your awareness, there's a good chance that your overall impact will be tipped toward the good side of the scale.

BEING PRESENT FOR PEOPLE

Not having enough time for the people in our lives, whether they are our friends, family, or co-workers, is a pervasive challenge for many of us today, especially for leaders with significant responsibilities in the workplace. We often feel as if we're on a fast-moving treadmill of daily, weekly, and monthly tasks, and we can barely keep up with the pace. In light of the overwhelming demand for our time and attention, we often don't prioritize our relationships. We tell ourselves, "Once I'm done with X, then I'll have time for you." But that time never comes.

If you want to be a strong leader, it's absolutely imperative that you find a way to make time for people, no matter how busy you are. That means making the effort to check in and connect with the key people in your life—friends, family, co-workers, team-mates. Doing so lets other people know that you value them. It builds trust. I believe that it is incumbent upon leaders to make even more effort than others to build relationships. As a leader, you should consider yourself a steward for the interconnections among the people within the many circles you're a part of.

I remember a story that one client told me about the work he was doing with his team. They were having trouble making progress on a big project. It seemed like no matter how long or how hard they worked, they never seemed to get any closer to their goal, and the deadline was fast approaching. He decided to try something completely out of character. On a Wednesday afternoon, he closed down the office and took everyone out for drinks. It gave everyone a chance to unwind and talk about something besides work. Plus, it was an indication from him that he valued everyone as human beings, and didn't think of them as robots. Even though, from one perspective, they didn't have the time to take a break from their work, it ended up supercharging their morale, and ultimately their productivity. By the end of the week, they had finished their project—and so they celebrated with another round of drinks.

In making time for others, quality is just as important as quantity. When you are with people, it is important that you are fully present, which in the smartphone age is becoming rarer and rarer. It's now commonplace for friends who are sharing a meal together to each have their phone on the table, paying as much attention to incoming texts as they are to the dinner conversation. I can't tell you the number of board meetings I've sat it on, where everyone in the room is in their own little universe, plugged into their phone or computer, and paying only partial attention to what's happening in the room. They simply aren't "present" and therefore the meetings are unproductive. People don't hear one another and little is accomplished. As bizarre as this state of affairs may seem, especially for those of us old enough to remember the pre-smartphone era, being fully present in our interactions with others has become a unique skillset. As a leader, you will be the one setting the tone for how people in your group or organization show up (or not) in everything from casual interactions to formal meetings. Your proficiency, then, at being fully present is crucial, and as with anything, takes practice.

BEING PRESENT TAKES COURAGE

Another way of thinking about "being present" is the practice of "mindfulness," which is a concept borrowed from Buddhism that has become very popular in the Western world over the past decade. Mindfulness, in essence, is being aware of as much of reality as possible—both inside and out.

I was recently invited to give a talk to a company in Myanmar, which is a predominantly Buddhist country. There were a handful of Buddhist monks in the audience, with their maroon robes and shaven heads. After my presentation, some of the monks told me how much they appreciated my approach to leadership development, and how relevant it seemed to their cultural worldview. One of the reasons they felt such connection with my work was my emphasis on the cultivation of presence, which they saw as mindfulness—a core principle of their Buddhist practice. As our conversation continued, one of them shared with me something I'll never forget. "Being present takes courage," the monk said, and continued without even the slightest hint of irony, "Sometimes the hardest thing you can do is to just do nothing."

That struck me. These monks, peaceful in their outer appearance and demeanor, are courageous individuals who have dedicated their lives to being fully present and awake in a world where there is constant pressure to be otherwise. Even in a country like Myanmar, where Buddhist monks make up a fair portion of the population, their chosen vocation is becoming rarer, and also more wrought with challenges from the culture at large. Today's world is all about action and results. The *last* thing we should be doing is simply taking the time to just be present—or so the world seems to scream. Whether you're doing hours of mindfulness practice like the monks, or simply making the effort to slow down and be more present in the workplace as a leader, you have to swim against a current rushing fast in the other direction. With countless demands for our attention, and an increasing pressure to deliver results, quickly, resisting the pressures to move too quickly or succumb to distraction takes a lot of courage.

Courage, as we've discussed, requires taking action in the face of resistance. It requires doing things that are unpopular or outside the box, knowing that there likely will be a lot of blowback. Think of the courage it takes Bill Gates, a man whose to-do list could fill a public library, to step away from it all for two weeks a year to take the time for reflection. My friend who took a risk and treated his team to drinks on a Wednesday afternoon exhibited real courage in doing so. Think of the courage required to take time every day away from your pressing deadlines to connect with the key people in your life. The best leaders find the wherewithal to be present. They accept it as part of the job.

THINK, DON'T OVERTHINK

We have talked at length in this chapter about the importance of being present, whether that takes the form of carefully thinking things through before taking action, or taking the time to connect with the key people in your life and work. But, as with all dimensions of Intelligent Leadership, there can be too much of a good thing. When it comes to staying present and being vigilant, the biggest danger is that we develop a tendency to *over*think situations and spend too much time in the "present moment" without moving into the future.

While there's no such thing as being too aware or too present, it is possible to get carried away and be lulled into inaction. In any given situation, there will always be a point at which you've done your due diligence and slowed down enough to become aware of the complexity you're facing. The time comes when you must just make a decision. If you get lost in the practice of awareness, and don't balance it with the other dimensions of IL, then you run the risk of being a very aware person who never gets anything done.

The same is true when making the time to be present for others. You need to find the right balance of connecting with others and also attending to the demands of your own life. I have worked with leaders who spend so much time worrying about others that they drive themselves crazy, and often don't have the time or space to make sure that they are getting what they need personally. You have to put on your own oxygen mask before attending to those around you. The key for this dimension, as with all the others, is striking the right balance.

THE MATRIX OF INTELLIGENT LEADERSHIP

At this point in our journey, you may be noticing how seamlessly interconnected are the many dimensions of Intelligent Leadership. In fact, as we get deeper into IL, it becomes difficult to introduce any new dimension without constantly referring to the others. The beauty of Intelligent Leadership is that each dimension contains within it hints of all the others.

Let's look, for example, at the connection between this Intelligent Leadership dimension and having the courage to execute with pride, passion, and precision. Being present requires courageous action, even if that "action" is actually ceasing to act. Similarly, when you are making the effort to infuse your actions with pride, passion, and precision, you will naturally bring a greater presence to everything you're doing.

We've also talked about the key role that the duty mindset plays in our capacity to be present. Indeed, the more present we are, the more connected we will be to the greater wholes that we are a part of.

Here's another: A key prerequisite to leveraging your gifts and addressing your gaps is taking the time and space to reflect on yourself. When you take this dimension of IL seriously, the natural result will be an increased awareness of how your actions are impacting others.

Bill Gates's Think Week is a great example of how being present interacts with the first dimension of Intelligent Leadership: thinking differently, thinking big. If you never take the time to step out of the constant stream of day-to-day tasks, you'll never have the space to actually think in new ways. Some of Gates's biggest, most innovative ideas came from simply making space for new thinking to emerge.

And then there's the vulnerability decision. In many ways, being present and being vulnerable are two sides of the same coin. There is no presence without vulnerability. And being vulnerable, in many ways, heightens your awareness of the impact that you're having on everyone around you.

Can you see how the dimensions all work together?

PRACTICING PRESENCE

One of the best phrases I've heard to describe our modern hyper-distracted state is "monkey mind." Like a wild monkey swinging through the jungle, our minds move from thought to thought, often in random order, quickly becoming distracted by every shiny object that enters our field of vision. Just pay attention to your train of thought during distracted periods of the day. You might set out to write an email to a colleague and twenty minutes later find that you are watching funny dog videos on your phone while you shop for new shoes on Amazon. These days, it can often feel as if "monkey mind" is a permanent state. Staying present is harder than ever.

Luckily for us, our monkey minds can be trained. There are countless practices and tools available today to help with the process of maintaining focus, staying present, and becoming more aware. I recommend that you find a set of tools that works for you. Below are a few principles and practices that I recommend for being more aware.

Less Is More

One of the biggest sources of distraction we face is overcommitment. We incorrectly assume that if we jam more items into our schedules, we will become more productive. In our attempts to honor the commitments we've made, we multitask when we would be better off staying focused exclusively on the task at hand. Predictably, our attempts to do more result only in a substandard job on more things. And our overcommitment keeps us in a perpetual cycle of distraction, which prevents us from being truly present for our work and our relationships.

I have found that one of the keys to staying present is what I call "the disciplined pursuit of less." None of us have infinite time and attention, so it's important for us to learn to get clear about what we should focus on and what we can cut out. This can be a challenging process, because it often seems like *everything* is important! But if you can get clear about your priorities, identify what is truly most important in your life, and then cut out anything that doesn't directly contribute to your bigger goals, you will become much more efficient with your time.

As a leader, you have to do this not only for yourself, but you also must set and maintain priorities for the groups you lead. You must be the one to keep things focused, right the ship when it gets off track, and keep everyone focused on the few simple things that will make the most impact. If you can achieve this degree of simplified focus, for yourself and your teams, you can accomplish far more than if you try to do too much.

Taking Time Just to Breathe

For millennia, human beings have been using the simple art of breathing to help maintain focus. Monks, meditators, yoga practitioners, and anyone who is just looking for a little reprieve from the mental onslaught that seems to characterize most of our lives all have turned to simple breathing techniques to center themselves and become more present.

I recommend taking time every day simply to listen to yourself breathe. It helps you both to prepare for the day ahead, and to calm down when you get overwhelmed. When you listen to yourself breathe, you are tuning into one single behavior, which enables you to block out the world, and slow things down to a manageable level. It can help you to avoid engaging in the negative thoughts and emotions that tend rise up quickly when you're under stress.

As you develop your ability to stay focused on your breath, you'll naturally begin to find that you have more bandwidth for other things. Your awareness will, in essence, expand. Your monkey mind never goes away, but as you develop your ability to focus, you'll be able to see the monkey mind for what it is, and keep it in its cage.

Remember, the Past Is Over

One of the biggest obstacles to being present is our natural human inclination to focus on the past. Most of us have at least a mild tendency to replay events or experiences, analyze mistakes, and agonize over things that might not have gone the way we wanted them to. If you pay attention to this tendency in yourself, you'll see that it's an addiction of sorts. Our minds are addicted to the past, an obsession that eats up a significant chunk of our bandwidth and keeps us from being aware of what's happening right now in the present.

When I catch myself in this cycle of past-addiction, I stop and take a moment to refocus myself on what is happening in the present moment. I remind myself that, as cliché as it sounds, you can't change what has happened in the past. All you have is *now*, and what you are going to do from *now on* to create your compelling future. Refocusing on the present in this way doesn't completely cure my addiction to the past, but it gives me a fighting chance of keeping those thoughts at bay, making more of my attention available to the present moment.

Take the Time to Listen

As we've discussed in this chapter, a big part of staying present is being more available in your relationships. A coaching colleague of mine, Avra Lyraki, uses a simple practice with her clients that I've also started to use with my own. She has found that most people she works with, many of whom are managers, don't spend enough time simply listening to the members of their teams. So she encourages them to structure time each week for "active listening." This can take many forms, but at a minimum, it requires you to make sure that you spend at least a short amount of time each week checking in with each member of your team (however you define it). In these sessions, it's crucial that you don't talk much, and give the other person the floor, paying close attention to what they tell you, whether it's personal or work-related.

This simple listening practice builds trust in your teammates. It makes them feel appreciated. It empowers them by letting them know that their thoughts and contributions are valuable. It's also a great way to stay in touch with the nuances and details of every aspect of your company or project. Taking time to check in with everyone provides you with valuable feedback and information.

Most importantly, taking the time to listen establishes your credibility as a leader. Leaders often make the mistake of thinking that their time is more important than anyone else's, but this breeds resentment. If you show that you value each and every person on your team, they will respect you more as a leader.

CHAPTER 8

Course Correction

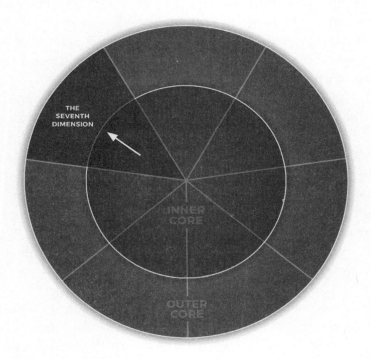

"Agility" has become a buzzword in both business and leadership circles these days. There are countless articles, podcasts, and blogs about how to become more agile, as a person or as an organization. I can't remember the last time I *didn't* hear "agility" mentioned as one of the top goals held by the executives and companies I work with. In fact, it's one of the most common qualities that people ask me to help them cultivate.

All this agility buzz makes sense, because change is constant—in business and otherwise. Life is speeding up, and so are most industry sectors. Change is occurring so fast that it's becoming increasingly difficult to make even short-term forecasts, and long-term business planning is becoming, for some, an exercise in futility. Those individuals and organizations thriving in this new world are those who are able to evolve, innovate, and change course. Agility isn't just a sexy concept; it's now a necessity.

One of the most rewarding interviews I did for my last book, *Cultural Transformations*, was with Cathy Benko, the vice chairman and managing principal of Deloitte Consulting LLP. Under Cathy's tutelage, Deloitte Consulting has gone from dead last to the top of their industry, much of which has been due to her willingness to constantly innovate their business model to adapt to the changing industry landscape. Cathy has an interesting take on agility, a word that she considers synonymous with innovation. During our interview, she recounted a story that speaks powerfully to the importance of constant innovation:

> I was recently talking to the editor in chief of *Fast Company* magazine about one of their annual features in which they name the 15 most innovative companies on the planet. I told him that while he's sitting on quite a franchise with the Top 15 list, I also think he's doing a disservice to his readers.
>
> Why is that? I did my own back-of-the-envelope longitudinal review of the last 10 years of the list, and it turns out they have featured a lot of flashes in the pan. Apple's always on it. Google's always on it. But there are also many organizations that were once considered innovative, but then in a year or two they were out of business.
>
> I suggested that there are a lot of existing companies in corporate America that I would argue are much more innovative than the "hot" companies that tend to make their list, but don't get credit for it. And I told him I could prove it. He asked me how. My answer? They're still here.

To Cathy Benko, change is such a constant that if you're not open to it, you're doomed. To survive as a leader or a company today, you have to be open to change. Agility, which I define as the ability to change course when the results and feedback you're receiving are pointing in new directions, is absolutely necessary.

But while agility and innovation are very sexy concepts—few would argue their importance—they are actually quite difficult to put into practice, both as an individual and especially as a group. The thing about change is that it requires you to, well, *change.* You have to stop doing one thing and start doing another. You have to break your habits and create new ones. When things aren't working, you have to change course. And as a leader, you need to help others do the same. This gets to the heart of the final dimension of Intelligent Leadership: course correction.

There's a famous Winston Churchill quote that I like to share with my clients: "Success is moving from failure to failure without loss of enthusiasm." But I always like to add a little twist. Rather than merely moving from failure to failure with a positive attitude, you must also *learn* something from each failure. That's the only way you'll ever change, and the only way you'll ultimately succeed. The greatest leaders are willing to correct their course, and they know how to inspire others to do the same. This is the key to being a truly agile leader.

Throughout this chapter, we're going to explore—in depth— how course correction is a quality of leadership. We'll discuss how you can start to embody a preference for—rather than resistance to—change, within your own life and within the groups and organizations you're a part of.

THE PSYCHOLOGY OF ADJUSTMENT

The biggest obstacle to mastering the art of course correction is our own psychology. Our brains are literally wired to create habits and norms, both in ourselves and in our groups, to make life easier. Just imagine what your life would be like if everything was constantly changing, and there were no routines. You wouldn't be able to get out of bed without your morning routine. And think of how hard it would be to navigate your way to work if you had to navigate a new route every day. Patterns and habits help make our lives stable, and stability is important for building an effective and productive life.

But sometimes stability can get in the way, and you need to override your wiring to create new habits. As the great eighteenth-century English writer Samuel Johnson wisely said, "The chains of habit are too weak to be felt until they are too strong to be broken." If you want to master the art of course correction, you must find a way to soften "the chains of habit" within yourself by cultivating a mindset that embraces change, rather than resists it. I call this mindset "the psychology of adjustment," and I've found that all great leaders possess this quality, at least to a certain degree. Without it, you will find yourself unable to correct course in those crucial moments where change is required.

The psychology of adjustment has four components, which we'll explore as we move through the chapter. They are both qualities of a change mindset and actions you can take to cultivate that mindset. Embodying these qualities is the key to course correction and crucial if you want to be an agile leader.

A Hunger for Constant Improvement

LeBron James is considered by many to be one of the greatest basketball players of all time. By the time his career is over, he will have achieved nearly everything there is to achieve in his sport and be among the all-time leaders in a remarkable number of statistical categories. When historians look back at his career, they will likely cite a variety of attributes that have contributed to his greatness: his athleticism, his competitive spirit, his extraordinary understanding of the game. But one quality, to me, stands out above all the others: his hunger for constant improvement.

As of this writing (in 2019), James has played in the National Basketball Association (NBA) for sixteen years. During that time, the game of basketball has gone through several different evolutions, and most of the players who started their careers alongside James have either retired or been made irrelevant. But James has evolved as the game has evolved. Every year, he adds a new component to his game in order to adapt to the changing landscape of the NBA. For example, over the past five years, the league has gone through a long-distance shooting revolution, and in order to make it in the NBA today, it's become almost a necessity to have a three-point shot. Earlier in his career, James was not a good three-point shooter. But, true to form, he has worked diligently to add this component of his game and is now among the league leaders in three-point shooting.

LeBron has, in abundance, the foundational element of "the psychology of adjustment." If you want to be an agile leader who can thrive in the chaotic world of constant flux that we're living in, you must cultivate a passion for consistent improvement. I'm not talking about simply a willingness to adapt when you're forced to. I'm talking about a *preference* for change. A love of learning. A desire for development. An interest in innovation. As a leader, you need to be the one who is actually seeking out opportunities for change, so—like LeBron James—you can always stay ahead of the curve.

As with all of the qualities we've explored in this book, it's okay if you don't already have a natural inclination toward change. If change scares you or intimidates you, there's no need to worry. You can cultivate a hunger for change, and once you start to experience it rise up in you naturally, you'll have at your disposal an important tool to break through the chains of habit. This passion, no matter how small it may be now, can grow to become a powerful source of strength when you are called upon to change course.

Take a moment to get in touch with your own hunger for development. Think of those moments in your own life where you have felt pulled by the possibility of becoming better, more, or different. No matter how "change averse" you may consider yourself to be, I'm sure you can find a part of you that feels otherwise.

(Why else would you be reading this book, and have made it this far along, in fact?) We each have within us a part that seeks out change and looks for opportunities to innovate. This part is like a small green shoot of a newly germinated seed, and your job is to cultivate it into a full-grown, thriving plant. When you embrace this part of yourself and let it grow, the lens through which you think about the process of change actually alters. Suddenly, you find yourself in the right mindset to approach any significant demand for change you may encounter.

Seeing Clearly

One of the most agile leaders I've worked with was a woman named Janet who is the head of a regional division of a major financial company. She is known for being an excellent problem solver. Janet is the person people call when things are going wrong. She has a talent for coming into any given situation, assessing the state of play, and then working with the key stakeholders to come up with innovative solutions that will help everyone move forward.

During our work together, I asked her what she felt was the key to her being so proficient at problem solving. Janet thought about it for a while and then said, "It's pretty simple actually. I make sure that I get the most accurate picture possible before taking action." I was intrigued by her answer and wanted to know more, so she continued, "You'd be surprised by how inaccurate are most people's perception of a given situation. Their picture is often clouded by all kinds of things—self-interest, personal bias, lazy thinking. If you can drill down and just see things clearly, for what they are, you're in a much better position to figure out the path forward."

Janet's sentiment reflects an extremely important element of the psychology of adjustment. Seeing clearly is absolutely crucial if you want to be in a position to course correct and set yourself and any group you're leading on the right path. The best leaders, like Janet, are uncompromising on this point. They don't accept gray areas, or unturned stones. To be an effective leader, you need to see a situation in the clearest possible light so that you can determine what needs to change, and how you might go about making that change.

Many people actually avoid clarity. They'd prefer to keep things vague and live in a state of denial about themselves and many of the situations they are involved in. The thing about clarity is that when you see a situation for what it really is, you find that you are compelled to make a change. Personally, you might find that there's a certain behavioral pattern that you've been engaged in that keeps getting in the way of your working relationships. Perhaps you have a lot of pride and are unwilling to ask for help in difficult situations. If you avoid seeing the dynamic for what it is, then you will continue to blindly operate the way you've always operated—at great expense to yourself and those around you. But if you are willing to face the situation for what it is and see it clearly, then you've made the first step toward dealing with it. You'll be compelled to make a change, and feel accountable for what you've seen.

As with having a hunger for improvement, be proactive about seeing clearly. As a leader you should always be striving to see the clearest possible picture, for yourself and others, in order to engage effectively in the process of change. If you don't do it, who else will?

A Willingness to Pivot

Seeing clearly is important, but unless you're willing to take action on what you see, then you won't progress. This is where the rubber meets the road. If you are able to see and acknowledge that something needs to change, then you need to take the courageous leap into action.

One of my favorite examples of this comes from the world of American college football. In the 2018 National Championship game, the heavily favored University of Alabama Crimson Tide, led by the legendary coach Nick Saban, were trailing their opponents, the University of Georgia Bulldogs, 13–0 at halftime. The Alabama offense had been completely stifled and their All-American quarterback, Jalen Hurts, was unable to execute their game plan against Georgia's defense.

So coach Saban did something radical in the second half. He opted to replace Hurts, one of the nation's top quarterbacks that year, with another player, Tua Tagliova, a first-year player who had barely played at all over the course of the season. He saw that Hurts's talents weren't working against Georgia, and that Tagliova had the right skillset to turn things around. And he was right. Led by Tagliova, Alabama orchestrated one of the greatest comebacks in college football history and ended up winning the game in overtime. Saban had the courage to do what only the greatest leaders do: he changed course. He faced the situation and saw it for what it was, then he made the necessary changes to correct it.

How often do people actually acknowledge they are on the wrong path, and then do something about it? This is a rare quality, because it's so much easier simply to maintain the status quo—to allow things to go on the way they have been. It takes significantly more effort to move things in a different direction. And you face incredible resistance, both within yourself and from those around you. The status quo is the status quo *for a reason*. It's strong and it's resistant to change. But if you want to be a leader—the kind of person who really makes a difference in the lives of those around you—then you have to be willing to stand up to that status quo and push it in a different direction.

There's a saying that history has always been moved forward by the heroic acts of individuals. People like Martin Luther King Jr. or Amelia Earhart refused to just accept things the way they were, and did something different. I'm not saying that in order to be a great leader you need to embody that degree of heroism, but you do need to muster the courage to pivot when the situation demands it. If you do so, you'll find that having courage to change becomes easier over time. You'll start to see "pivot" moments as what they are: natural points in the evolution of your own life, or the life of your organization, where change is ready to happen, and you're the one who needs to step up and do what needs to be done to facilitate that change process.

Living Outside Your Comfort Zone

The final component of the psychology of adjustment is the willingness to live outside your comfort zone. Once you've seen a situation for what it is and decided to take action based on that information, you're going to find yourself in new territory. You'll experience this personally when you are developing a new habit or behavior, and culturally when you instigate a change in the way your organization functions.

When you make changes this big, the experience is intense! You're exposed. You aren't sure how to act, and that can feel raw and unfamiliar. Remember, this is new ground you're treading, so you don't have much experience to rely on, and no reference point to give you the confidence you would normal have to help you move forward. This is what it feels like to live outside your comfort zone.

But if you want to be a leader of change, an agile person who can catalyze the evolution of your group or organization, you have to find a way to become comfortable outside your comfort zone. I'm not suggesting that you can ever *feel* comfortable in this new, unknown territory. That's literally impossible. But you can start to understand the dynamics of change, so that operating outside your comfort zone doesn't shock you. You can anticipate the uncomfortability and prepare yourself for it so you don't retreat or backtrack.

Many people, when they step outside their comfort zone, are overcome by fear and anxiety. They become crippled and don't know where to turn. But the best leaders find a way to withstand those emotions and move forward anyway. Cathy Benko, whom I mentioned earlier in this chapter, is someone who has mastered the art of living outside her comfort zone. I think the perspective that has supported her ability to live so far outside her comfort zone is seeing herself as a "perpetual work in progress." She's no longer bound by any significant attachment to the way things are because she's grown to expect change. She expects things to be new and uncomfortable. That's the only way that growth happens.

Putting Them All Together

Together, the four components of the psychology of adjustment create a mindset that embraces change, rather than resists it. When you are hungry for constant improvement, you are compelled to view every situation with the utmost clarity. When you're seeing clearly, you're able to determine what's working and what needs to be tweaked, changed, or abandoned altogether. If you have the courage to act on what you see and change course, you'll find yourself in a new reality outside your comfort zone. If you can handle the challenging dynamics of operating in unknown territory, then you'll develop a preference for seeking out new innovations and opportunities. Rinse and repeat.

A CULTURE OF INNOVATION

Embracing the psychology of adjustment as an individual is a difficult but achievable task. Bringing this change mindset to an entire group, company, or organization is without question more challenging. The collective resistance to change can often be much more pernicious and difficult to overcome than the resistance within a single individual. Status quos are stronger in groups, and habits are often more difficult to break. That's why it's so important for leaders to embody a psychology of adjustment.

As a leader, you are the one who sets the tone for your greater wholes, and if you set the example as someone who embraces rather than resists appropriate change, others will follow suit. As you begin to exercise this part of yourself, you'll find that your preference for change starts to become contagious. Your love for learning, your willingness to change, your demand for clarity, and your preference for new, unknown opportunities will start to create a "culture of innovation" within the groups you lead.

All of us, deep down, want things to be better, to improve, even if we're stuck in old habits. We just need a little push or a little pull. We need someone to show us that there is another way to do things, and that it's okay to change, even if it's intimidating or scary at first. That's where you, as the leader, come in. Your relationship to change will inspire those around you. That's why it's so crucial that you master the art of course correction.

Collective Unintelligence

I was recently contracted to work with a company that had just gone through a messy merger process, and was experiencing negative fallout as a result. Communications had been poor and the strategic plan for how to roll out the merger had been very sloppy. As a result, people throughout every level of the organization were experiencing tremendous frustration. Many felt undermined by the process and had lost trust in the leadership of the company.

They wanted me to work with the key stakeholders to assess and then figure out how to repair the damage that been done to the culture of the organization. My first move was to interview everyone who had been involved in planning the merger. What I discovered was shocking.

It turns out that no one involved in the process from either of the two companies actually thought the merger was a good idea. However, because each person thought others were behind it, they had supported the merger against their better judgment. In interview after interview, the answers were all the same. It turns out that everyone "in the room" wanted a different outcome, but because they were afraid to go against the perceived will of the group, they didn't speak up. The status quo of the collective was so strong that a group of people all agreed to pursue an outcome that none of them wanted.

Once we were able to identify this collective delusion, we were able to reestablish trust among the key stakeholders of the company, which served as the foundation for repairing the company culture. The merger was a done deal at that point, but from this base of trust, we were able to identify a productive path forward for the new company.

DON'T OVERCORRECT

When my kids were growing up, I had the opportunity to coach several of their sports teams, both basketball and baseball. One of the most important jobs as a coach is helping to correct your players—their form, their decisions, and their understanding of the game. The trick to good coaching, I discovered, is learning when to step in and correct the players, and when to allow them to figure things out for themselves. Overcorrecting could undermine their confidence and stop their progress before it has a chance to really flourish.

There is a similar balance required when it comes to this dimension of Intelligent Leadership. In your efforts to be open to change, find the areas that need to be improved, and then take action to correct the course, it's important that you don't *over*correct. I've worked with hundreds of clients who take course correction to an extreme and end up full of anxiety, always searching for problems that need to be corrected and driving themselves (and everyone around them) crazy. There are plenty of situations where it may seem like things are "off" at first, but over time the perceived problem tends to work itself out, or a bump in the road turns out to be a blessing in disguise. So it's important to temper your course correction with a dose of "wait and see."

THE ULTIMATE DIMENSION

While all of the IL dimensions work together to form one dynamic perspective, course correction may be the one that best ties all of the others together. If you are going to master the art of course correction, you will need to have all the other dimensions firing at a high level.

1. **Thinking Differently, Thinking Big**
   If you are striving to achieve this, you will inherently be oriented toward consistent improvement and change. You will be seeking

out the opportunities to change course to make your impact even greater.

2. **The Vulnerability Decision**

   Similarly, if you want to embody the psychology of adjustment, vulnerability is absolutely crucial. You need to be willing to open yourself up to the feedback of others, and be vulnerable enough to acknowledge mistakes and flaws in order to correct them.

3. **Having a Mindset of Entitlement versus a Mindset of Duty**

   When you burst the bubble of your entitlement and embrace a duty mindset, you're able to see the biggest possible context for your actions. Having this bigger picture empowers you to better identify the areas that need improvement and set yourself on the right course. In many ways, the duty mindset amplifies your ability to see clearly.

4. **Leveraging Your Gifts and Addressing Your Gaps**

   Similarly, learning to identify your gifts and gaps, and then responding correctly, is a crucial step in being able to course correct effectively. Much like not overcorrecting, you don't want to overlook your strengths and always seek out your weaknesses.

5. **Having the Courage to Execute with Pride, Passion, and Precision**

   As we've discussed at length in this chapter, course correction requires a tremendous degree of courageous action. Identifying the opportunities for change is only the first step in the process. Taking action is what makes it a reality.

6. **Staying Present and Being Vigilant**

   Finally, staying present and being vigilant is crucial to being in a constant state of improvement. You must be as awake as possible to be able to make accurate decisions about when—and when not—to change course.

CORRECTING YOUR COURSE

Course correction is both a mindset and an action. As an action, course correction is what you do in the moment, when you need to pivot. As a mindset, it's a way of life: you are aware that you and the world around you are in a state of constant evolution, and that perspective allows you to stay balanced in the face of inevitable change.

In both cases, course correction takes practice. Yes, you can cultivate course correction as both an action and a mindset. Even the most stubborn among us can learn to become agile. And the most innovative, change-friendly leaders can, by definition, become even more effective in their willingness and ability to course correct.

Below are a series of igniter behaviors that will help you cultivate your own psychology of adjustment. They are tools you can use to pivot in any given situation, and they are principles that will help you to become a more agile leader.

Refocus on the Present

One of the keys to effective course correction is being able to see yourself and any situation as clearly as possible so you can make an accurate assessment of what steps may or may not need to be taken. For this reason, I recommend that you apply the sixth dimension of Intelligent Leadership, staying present and being vigilant, so you can be fully aware of what's going on around you. As you begin to develop your own "psychology of adjustment," make sure you are staying as present as possible. You can use the tools laid out in the last chapter, like breathing or other mindfulness techniques, or you can invent your own. The key here is to recognize that your ability to adapt to the changes around you is dependent upon your ability to stay fully present.

Do What's Right, Not What You Think Is Right

Human beings are stubborn creatures. And leader types, who have a lot of boldness and confidence, are often the most stubborn. This is a positive attribute in situations where one needs to stay on course in the face of overwhelming obstacles and challenges. But the unwillingness to pivot can be a big liability in situations where agility is required. I have a little practice that I do personally, and also invite my clients to do, whenever I'm in a challenging situation where I perceive a change might need to be made. The practice is this: I take a moment to question my own judgment. I don't undermine myself in that overly self-critical way. I simply ask myself, "Are my thoughts on this situation based on what *I* think is right or what is actually right?" Sometimes, if appropriate, I will also do a quick poll of those I'm working with, to help further clarify the situation. It's a simple exercise, but it's effective. Just taking a moment to reflect honestly on the course you've chosen opens you up to the possibility of change.

Surround Yourself with Honest, Courageous People

This is crucial: as a leader, you need to make sure that the people around you are willing to give you honest feedback, even if it directly contradicts your own thoughts or choices. Surrounding yourself with honest, courageous people will give you access to a strong group intelligence, which is almost always greater, richer, and more complex than the mind of even the most brilliant individual. Tapping into that collective mind will always give you a fuller picture of any given situation, reveal new and creative solutions, and position you to make the best possible choice about how to move forward.

If you want to have an atmosphere of honesty and courage within your team, it's important to choose the right people. With whatever degree of choice you have over who will be part of your team, do your best to select for this quality of fearless honesty. Once you have your team on board, it's crucial that you, as a leader, create an atmosphere in which honest feedback is not only accepted, it's encouraged. Don't let your own pride create a sense of intimidation amongst your team members. Your openness will set the tone for the rest of your group, and create a culture of open feedback, constructive criticism, and constant innovation.

CHAPTER 9

It's Not About You

The Inseparable Relationship Between Leadership and Culture

When you pick up a book like this one, your motives for doing so are likely to be at least somewhat selfish. I don't mean "selfish" in a negative way. I mean that you are probably interested in improving yourself so you can be a better leader and achieve something personally. To me, this is a noble motive. Personal improvement, in nearly any context, is a good thing. As you better yourself, your life improves. But it's more than that, too: Your improvement as an individual is inseparable from the overall betterment of every group or project of which you're a part, whether it's a family, a team, a company, or—if you want to go really big—the human race. As we discussed in our exploration of the duty mindset, we all belong within a vast configuration of greater wholes. So when we develop, everything our lives touch does as well.

For me this is the Trojan horse of Intelligent Leadership. You might initially be compelled by the promise of improving your leadership capacity so you can get a promotion or be more personally successful. But at the end of the day, the truly great leaders understand that this development is not really about *them*. They learn—and eventually internalize—that the most important effect their leadership development can have is on the *cultures* that they are a part of. Leaders are stewards of culture, whether they like it or not.

So what is culture? That's a difficult question to answer, because culture, by its nature, is very subtle and hard to define. So I'm going to use a metaphor from anatomy to explain.

I sometimes work out with a personal trainer, and she's always emphasizing to me the importance of doing a proper warm-up before every exercise session. In particular, she stresses the importance of loosening up my "myofascial tissue." For those of you who aren't up on the latest fitness warm-up trends, myofascial tissue is an extremely thin, nearly invisible layer of fibrous tissue that surrounds all of our muscles and bones. Despite being extremely thin, it's very strong. It literally holds our bodies together, and protects our muscles and bones. Imagine it like a net, and if there are knots or bunches of net that aren't moving freely, the bones and muscles underneath the net are literally caught, or bound up, unable to function efficiently. So, if you want to unlock greater movement in your body, my trainer loves to say, you need to first loosen up the myofascial tissue. This is usually accomplished by the painful process of slowly massaging the key points in our musculoskeletal system with a hard foam roller. It might hurt, but it works. And I'm now a believer in the crucial role that myofascial tissue plays in the overall health of the body.

I think of "culture" as the myofascial tissue of any organizational structure—whether that structure is small like a family or a team, or massive, like a multinational company or even a nation. The culture of any group is usually invisible to its members, largely because it's not just one thing. It's a conglomeration of all the shared values and beliefs, relational structures, and rules (both conscious and unconscious) about what is right and wrong, good and bad, acceptable and unacceptable. Like myofascial tissue, culture holds your organization together, and shapes nearly every dimension of it.

Culture is something you *feel*, a subtle attitude or space that permeates the atmosphere of your home, or workplace, or city. And funnily enough, when things are good, it's harder to notice. When your culture is humming, it positively accentuates everything else about your organization or group. A clue to assessing the health of your organization's culture is the degree of lightness or creativity infusing everything and everyone in your group. The members experience greater satisfaction, and the bottom-line results that you're collectively able to achieve improve.

The opposite can also be true. When there's something wrong with your culture—like when your myofascial tissue is rigid, or all bound up and needing a good rolling—it can feel like a heaviness or tension in the air of your organization. Morale is low, infighting and power struggles are common, and people are more focused on what they can get out of the company than what they can give, all of which usually leads to decreased productivity—and profitability.

One example that comes to mind that helps make the concept of culture visible is the culture of New York City following the attacks of September 11. Countless people commented that the tragedies of that day created a palpable sense of common purpose that brought people together. The usual barriers people erect around themselves were dropped. Strangers felt like brother and sisters. Those events, at least temporarily, shifted the culture of an entire city, and it mobilized people into action. The sudden change in the experience of their own culture revealed to New Yorkers something they probably hadn't really thought much about before. Now, it's important to know that it doesn't take a precipitous event or a tragedy to make culture visible, or to create a positive culture in a family, business, or nation. I share this example simply as a way to get you thinking about how to "see" culture in your own life.

IT STARTS AT THE TOP

It goes without saying that culture is important to the health and profitability of any organization. That's why more and more companies and nonprofits are paying attention to this dimension of the workplace and devoting resources to learning about the subtle dynamics that determine their culture's vibrancy (or lack thereof). I've spent a great deal of my career working with companies to assess the health of their culture, and to develop plans for how to improve it. Through a series of surveys (see the sidebar "Measuring the 'Five Cultures of Culture'" later in this chapter), we measure the cultural health of an organization. We then diagnose the problems and prescribe actionable solutions. Time and time again, I've found that one key factor predicts the health and vibrancy of an organizational culture more than anything else: leadership.

Remember our definition of leadership from the book's introduction? We talked about it as being an example for others to follow. This gets right to the heart of why leadership has such a significant influence on culture. If you are at or near the top of any group, your behavior, your perspective, and your actions will have more impact than anyone else's on the culture of your organization. Whether you like it or not, you *model* the shared values, perspectives, and ultimately, the behavior of everyone else. The best leaders are aware of this influence—and they understand just how important it is to facilitate and inspire a strong culture through their own example. My friend and colleague Eddie Machaalani, the founder and CEO of the ecommerce company Bigcommerce, sums it up beautifully:

> Your company culture starts from the top. It starts with the CEO first and foremost. You can't fake a company culture if the CEO doesn't live by the core values of the organization.

So what, exactly, does a strong and vibrant culture look like? This of course, varies depending on the circumstances. A healthy culture will look different in a nonprofit organization, for instance, than it will in a Silicon Valley tech start-up. The cultural feel of a company based in Denmark will likely be quite different from one in Chile. Culture is, by its very nature, hard to pin down and reduce to simple parts. That said, there are some universal elements of a strong culture that are worth exploring. In fact, I've found that all seven dimensions of Intelligent Leadership are also dimensions of a healthy culture.

I don't mean to suggest that these seven dimensions are the definitive qualities of a strong culture. That would require another book (or two) to explore. But what I would like to discuss as we come to the end of our journey together is how each dimension of Intelligent Leadership expresses itself at the level of culture. If you are exhibiting these dimensions, then you will naturally inspire similar qualities in the culture you lead.

As we work our way through each dimension, I'll be using real-world examples of how leaders impact their company culture based on stories from my last book, *Cultural Transformations*, in which I interviewed fourteen of the world's top CEOs about the relationship between leadership and culture.

Let's begin with the first dimension, "Thinking Differently, Thinking Big."

Measuring the "Five Cultures of Culture"

Like the individual, culture also has many dimensions. I've identified what I call "Five Cultures of Culture" within an organization, and I've developed tools to measure the health and vibrancy of each in order to get a 360-degree view of the overall strength of any given organization's culture. Each of these five cultures is an avenue for exploring the infinite depth of the relationships, shared values, and core principles that define your organization's inner core:

1. **Capability Culture:** Cultivating the skills and capacities of people within an organization. Are people developing their inner and outer core?
2. **Commitment Culture:** The amount of passion that members of an organization feel for its vision, mission, and brand.
3. **Alignment Culture:** The level of clarity and unity around the overarching mission of an organization. How aligned are people with this big vision?
4. **Individual Performance Culture:** The degree to which there is a shared value of excellence and execution exhibited by members of an organization.
5. **Team Performance Culture:** The amount of collaboration present when getting things done. Do people work together?

If you're interested in learning more about how we measure the Five Cultures of Culture at the level of an organization, please visit johnmattone.com/booktools.

ENCOURAGING INNOVATION

There may be no better example of how leadership can set the tone for a company culture than how Steve Jobs led Apple during his tenure there. Indeed, his Think Different ethos has defined Apple's company culture for decades. To this day, when you walk into an Apple Store, you feel that sense of newness, cutting-edge design, and outside-the-box thinking. Jobs's own willingness always to think bigger has been infused into every corner of Apple, from its products to its futuristic corporate headquarters in Mountain View, California. It's this culture of innovation that has kept Apple at the forefront of the personal technology industry for decades.

So how do you create a culture of thinking differently and thinking big?

According to North Face founder Hap Klopp, one of the key ingredients is cultivating an environment where experimentation—and failure—are encouraged. Klopp, who ran the trendsetting outdoor gear company for twenty years, cites the willingness to fail as one of the primary reasons for North Face's success. Fear of failure is one of the biggest reasons why people don't venture outside of their comfort zone, try on new ways of thinking, or dare to think big. But if failure is something that you, as a leader, embrace in yourself and also encourage in others, you'll create an environment that is much more conducive to new ways of thinking. People will be more willing to take risks and try on new perspectives, which are two of the primary ingredients that drive innovation.

Another important part of creating a thinking big culture is fostering an environment in which your employees or team members are connected to a deeper sense of purpose. Klopp feels a passion for helping people connect with the natural world through outdoor adventure. He's built his personal mission into the mission of the company, and made sure to keep it front and center in everything they do. Thus, the company ethos has made the North Face's products attractive to adventure seekers all over the world, and has also attracted countless talented employees to join the company and inspired them to think bigger than just the bottom line.

Not every culture needs to have the same innovative feel as Apple or the mission-driven appeal of the North Face. But if you, as the leader, are willing to think big and encourage others to do the same, the culture you build will have a unique, innovative quality that will compel others and keep everyone always looking toward the future.

VULNERABILITY IS CONTAGIOUS

Trust is the lifeblood of a strong culture, and separates healthy cultures from unhealthy ones. If people trust one another, then communication lines are open and individuals are focused primarily on what binds them, rather than what separates them. If trust is absent, then a culture devolves into a dog-eat-dog atmosphere where everyone is fundamentally in it for themselves. This creates a toxic environment within your group or organization, negatively impacting effectiveness, productivity, and profitability.

The key to building trust within your organization is vulnerability. People willing to let down their guard with each other immediately experience trust between them. It is almost miraculous. Think of a person with whom you have a negative relationship. It could be someone in your workplace or elsewhere. Imagine if you were to approach them one day and let them know about a challenge you're facing, asking for their input. It would be difficult, but I'm willing to bet that it would make them trust you more, and have a significantly positive impact on your relationship.

Vulnerability is like a secret weapon that you, the leader, can use to heighten the trust in your organizational culture. The default setting in most organizational cultures is lack of trust, with people holding their cards close to their chest. Because most of us tend to equate vulnerability with weakness, building trust through vulnerability can be difficult.

You may recall the example from Chapter 3 about the CEO who was trying to grow his company and, in order to do so, had to start delegating more responsibility to others. At first, he didn't want to open up to anyone about the challenges he was facing—he came from the John Wayne school of leadership, after all. He was having a hard time trusting his employees enough to begin to bring them into the management of the company. But when he dared to be vulnerable with others, he found that he had been overlooking an incredible amount of support among his employees. He began to trust them enough to allow them to be responsible for making the company grow, and they trusted him to be hands-off and let them do it.

You, as the leader, must be the chief vulnerability officer of your organization. Through your own example, you can create an environment in which people don't see vulnerability as weakness. You can destroy the John Wayne mentality that keeps people apart, trusting no one but their own selves, and avoiding collaboration. Vulnerability brings people together and amplifies what you can all achieve.

A CULTURE OF DUTY

In many ways, entitlement is the biggest enemy of a strong and vibrant culture. People whose primary mindset is one of entitlement are inherently self-involved and have little interest in contributing to the greater mission of an organization. On a large scale, this "What's in it for me?" mentality erodes the very core of any group. Culture is, by definition, a collective phenomenon. If your team members are only focused on themselves, then a culture becomes toxic.

That's why it's so important for leaders to cultivate a sense of duty, in both themselves and their organization. You, as the leader, need to find ways to shift the collective focus from "me" to "we." I'm not talking subverting the interests of the individual for those of the company. The best cultures are those in which the members see their own self-interest as *synonymous* with that of the organization. The duty mindset, remember, is seeing yourself in a much bigger context, and understanding how you and your actions contribute to the many greater wholes that you are a part of. If you can create an environment in which everyone understands his or her role in your organization, and feels valued and empowered in it, then you'll unlock a profound degree of team spirit in your culture.

A strong example of a "duty" culture comes from the world of professional basketball. Since 2014, the Golden State Warriors have been the gold standard of excellence in the NBA. They have amassed three world championships over a five-year period, and have been to a record five straight NBA finals. Whether or not you're a fan of the "Dubs," as their fans call them, it's hard to deny that they have cultivated a strong team culture, where each member of the team, no matter how big a star he as an individual may be, feels a sense of duty to the greater whole. The world of professional sports is full of big money, big fame, and big egos, which often get in the way of building a strong team culture. The Warriors are no exception. In fact, they have some of the most talented players in the world on their roster, some of whom could be the top player on many other teams in the league. But instead of money, fame, or ego getting in the way, each member of the Warriors has bought in to the team mantra: "Strength in Numbers." They have all found a way to put the success of the team above their own personal glory. How does this display itself? Players have agreed to sacrifice their own playing time, statistics, and even salaries, in order to contribute to the harmony of their team. And the results speak for themselves. The Warriors have been able to achieve more together than any other team in history, breaking their own record season after season, and individual players are each hitting and breaking personal records because of the strength of who they are as a team.

So how do you instill a sense of duty into your culture? The most important component, of course, is that you—as a leader—are demonstrating the duty mindset yourself. But it's also important to make sure that you are putting the right people, with the right mindset, in other positions of leadership. Kathy Mazzarella is CEO of Graybar, a Fortune 500 industrial and electrical distribution company. One of the primary qualities she looks for when filling leadership positions within her company is a sense of obligation to the betterment of the company. Do candidates possess a duty mindset—an ability to see themselves as an important part of a much larger whole? Or are they mostly just in it for themselves? Mazzarella says that all the talent in the world can't replace this sense of duty when it comes to finding strong leaders. And using this criterion for hiring leaders has worked for Graybar. The company's employee retention and satisfaction levels are industry-leading, and it's not uncommon for people to stay on with the company for thirty or forty years. In fact, Mazzarella herself started working for Graybar when she was nineteen years old, and stuck with the company for thirty-five years, rising through the ranks and eventually becoming one of only a handful of female Fortune 500 CEOs in the world.

Whether you're a professional sports team or a large industrial corporation, duty is an absolutely critical ingredient in building a strong and lasting culture. Duty is the mindset that binds culture together, and it's your job as a leader to set that tone for everyone involved.

A CULTURE THAT AMPLIFIES

In the same way that individual potential is maximized by learning to address your gaps and leverage your gifts, an organization's culture can be supercharged when weaknesses are dealt with constructively and strengths are both sought out and amplified. I've encountered organizational cultures that didn't do this well, and the result is an atmosphere in which improvement was virtually impossible. People would get defensive about critical feedback and felt underutilized and underappreciated. But when the opposite is true, in a culture where strengths and weaknesses are handled effectively, everyone in the organization is lifted up and feels deeply empowered to maximize their own potential.

If you, the leader, are able to hold the right mindset in relationship to people's weaknesses, then you can set the tone for a more wholesome, development-oriented culture. Remember, the key to addressing your gaps effectively is understanding that none of us are perfect—that we are all in the process of perpetually improving. If that's the cultural attitude of your organization, then people will feel less defensive and more open to addressing their gaps. In fact, they will seek them out in order to find ways to improve themselves. If you are setting the right course at the top, then you can have an entire culture of constant improvement.

One of the biggest hallmarks of a strong company culture is the degree to which people seek out and then empower the unique gifts and talents of everyone in the company. Rohit Mehrotra, founder and CEO of one of the fastest-growing tech-service companies in the U.S., CPSG Partners, says that one of his best traits as a leader is finding the part of every one of his employees that is extraordinary. He doesn't accept the fact that only some people have the potential for greatness, and often hires people with unique backgrounds and skillsets that other companies might overlook. Mehrotra believes that if you are willing to look in the right places, you can find greatness in anyone. The key is to find it, and then support it.

You, as the leader, are primarily responsible for infusing your culture with this process-oriented perspective. If you can help people to see themselves—their flaws and their talents—as part of one big continuum, you'll create the foundation for a culture that values improvement over everything else. That's an inspiring group to be a part of.

CREATING A CULTURE OF COURAGEOUS ACTION

One quality I look for in the "air" of any organization is a sense of liveliness and activity. Does it feel as if something is *happening*? Is everyone engaged and focused on creating concrete results? Are people results-oriented and rewarded for taking the right kind of action on behalf of the organization's goals? Does it feel as if everyone knows that it's game time and is acting accordingly? These are tangible qualities that reflect the degree to which a culture values courageous action.

Taking action and executing on your plans and visions is difficult. It takes courage and it takes focus. You as the leader set the tone for your culture in this regard. What is your own relationship to taking action? Are you consistently stepping outside your comfort zone? Do you take concrete steps toward progress, even in the face of resistance? As the leader of an organization, you have to be more courageous than anyone else. If you're taking this responsibility on your shoulders, it will infuse your culture with the same qualities.

You may recall from Chapter 6 that courageous action has several dimensions: pride, passion, and precision. Each is both an individual and a cultural virtue. There is a profound difference between groups that take pride in their work and those that don't—usually the difference is between long-term success and failure. You want your organizational culture to inspire everyone to feel proud to be a member. You want it to be a place that everyone wants to show off to the world. The identity of the company and the identity of the individual reflect one another, and as the leader, you want *pride* to be the characteristic shining out into the world. That's what compels others to want to come on board!

Does your culture inspire passion in people? Passion is the energy of a culture. The degree of passion that people feel for the work they're doing together, or for the mission of the organization, is ultimately what drives success or failure. It's your job, as a leader, to inspire that passion. This can be done through example—your own passion is contagious. You can also fuel passion within the culture of your organization by creating an atmosphere in which everyone is encouraged to connect with their personal passion in a way that contributes to the whole. Are you empowering people to discover what makes them tick and finding ways to harness those passions for the good of the organization?

Precision is reflected in the quality and efficiency of your culture. Are there clear standards within your organization and are they clearly articulated? Do people stay focused on their tasks and overarching goals? Strong cultures, while not rigid, maintain an atmosphere of focus in which everyone's time and energy is valued and maximized. There's an attention to detail that permeates everything from the ways meetings are run to broad-scale communications.

As a leader, being willing to take courageous action in a way that displays pride, passion, and precision will have a profound effect on everyone around you. Your organization will buzz like a beehive, and will be filled with energy, focus, and a collective determination to accomplish your goals. This energy will attract others and amplify your collective impact.

WORKING AS ONE

I'm a big fan of team sports. I love the way it brings people together, if even for a short period of time, aligned in a kind of collective harmony. This is especially the case in the sport of basketball, which, when played at the highest level, resembles the improvisational genius of jazz. When things are really clicking, each of the five players on the court become something more than just individuals. They are in sync with one another to a degree that those who've experienced it can only describe as "being in the flow."

In his 2006 book, *Sacred Hoops*, legendary NBA coach Phil Jackson talks about the psychological dynamics that he credits for his success both as a player and a coach. Jackson, who won more titles than any other coach in NBA history (11 of them, with two different teams), was also a practicing Zen Buddhist, and used a variety of mindfulness techniques with his players to help them find focus and come together as a team. By learning to stay in the moment, Jackson's players were able to tune out the distractions and chaos that are often the norm in high-stakes professional sports and find a focus that amplified their abilities, both individually and collectively.

Jackson was able to get some of the game's greatest super-stars—household names like Michael Jordan, Kobe Bryant, and Shaquille O'Neal—to lay down their own egos and play *as one* with their teammates. Many who played for Jackson talk about how their mindfulness practices would help them tap into a collective intelligence. During a game, they would be able to anticipate one another's movements to an uncanny degree. Like a flock of sparrows moving seamlessly together in the sky, the heightened awareness among the players enabled these teams to achieve a harmony that resulted in some of the most successful teams in history.

Jackson's mindfulness approach to basketball is a great example of how staying present and being vigilant shows up at the level of culture. When everyone on a team is striving to be as present as possible, the potential for what you can achieve is exponential. Things move faster when you're not distracted, and you are able to share a perspective that is more complex, fulfilling, and dynamic than any of your individual perspectives. When you make the effort to tune out all the distractions, both from within your own heads and from the world around you—and do it together as a team—you will communicate more effectively, take more into account, make fewer mistakes, and ultimately produce more as a team.

CORRECTING YOUR COLLECTIVE COURSE

Kris Canekeratne is one of the most inspiring executives I've had the pleasure of working with. Canekeratne is the CEO and founder of Virtusa, an IT services company based out of Massachusetts and his native Sri Lanka. Virtusa has experienced tremendous success as a company over the past two decades, and Canekeratne attributes this primarily to the culture of constant innovation that he and his co-workers have built.

The landscape of IT services has changed dramatically since Virtusa was founded in 1996. Since those early days of the internet, countless competitors have come and gone. From the very beginning, Canekeratne knew that in order to stay relevant in this highly competitive atmosphere, he and his team would need to build a love for change into the very fabric of their company culture. He encouraged everyone in the organization—from the highest levels of management to the entry-level employees—to share ideas about how to evolve or even change the business, no matter how dramatic. He coined a motto, "When you stop evolving, you fail," and he worked diligently to keep everyone focused on constant improvement. Thanks to his efforts, Virtusa embodies a culture of course correction perhaps more fully than any company I've encountered. As a natural result of their cultural attitude, they've been able to reinvent themselves several times over throughout their twenty-plus years in business. By changing, they've remained an industry leader in one of the most competitive and fastest-changing sectors on the planet.

Organizational agility is more important today than it ever has been. In order for any company to be more than just a flash in the pan, it is crucial that leaders create a culture in which course correction is not only encouraged, but a top priority. As a leader, it's on you to create an environment in which everyone is always looking for opportunities to improve, and where people are encouraged to bring new ideas. You don't want to foster a culture in which people are afraid to suggest new directions. That's a recipe for failure. Everyone in your organization should feel a passion for the success of the company and be empowered to play a role in moving it forward.

Agile leadership takes a high degree of maturity. You can't be proud. You have to be vulnerable and open. You have to develop excellent communication and engender in everyone involved a high degree of collective passion for your greater mission. If you can pull this off, then you'll set up your whole organization for long-term success. You'll have a culture of constant correction, improvement, and evolution.

AS YOU GO, SO GO WE ALL

I hope I've made it abundantly clear just how deeply connected are leadership and culture. The two are, quite literally, two sides of the same coin. Don't believe me? Google the top ten organizations to work for and take a look at their leadership teams. I promise that you'll find a direct correlation between the elements that make their culture so attractive, and the conscious actions of their leaders.

If you want to be a truly great leader, it's absolutely crucial that you embrace and embody the powerful connection between yourself and the cultures you're a part of. The inner core qualities that you cultivate in yourself will deeply shape the cultural qualities of your organization. At a certain level, they are, without a doubt, one and the same.

Taking on this cultural imperative is a big responsibility, for sure. People are depending on you. There's no time off from being a leader, a model, an influencer of others. People are always looking toward you as an example, and how you are will, to a large extent, set the tone for everyone around you.

Take heart: the best leaders find this reality inspiring. By daring to take on the mantle of Intelligent Leadership, your actions, attitudes, and behavior will have a concrete impact on the world around you. As you go, so go we all. I can't think of a more powerful motivation to be the best possible leader—and person—you can be.

CHAPTER **10**

Conclusion

The Paradox of Change

One of the first questions that I ask my clients when we start to work together is: "Do you think that in order to be a great leader, you need to operate in a way that conflicts with your personal preferences?" It's kind of a trick question, because you can answer it accurately in two opposite ways. On one hand, great leadership is inside all of us, even if deeply buried. We just need to nurture and cultivate these innate qualities so that they begin to rise to the surface and guide our thoughts and actions.

But on the other hand, even if great leadership is inside of us as potential, who we are—our preferences, behavior, thinking patterns—may not be a reflection of that greatness. It is obscured and overshadowed by less desirable qualities and habits. So in order to actually become a great leader, we need to change. We need to change the way we think, the way we act, the way we interact. Essentially, we need to become a new person, even if that person is a better version of the person we already are.

This is the paradox of change. It requires us to become something new and different, but also more deeply who we already are.

As you've engaged with each of the dimensions of Intelligent Leadership, I'm sure that you've experienced this paradox directly yourself. As we discussed the vulnerability decision, for example, you might have experienced a deep resonance with the power of opening up to yourself and to others. You may have even seen how vulnerability has helped you in your own life. But you may also have been intimidated by this quality, even avoided it for most of your life. And you may have seen that if you were to bring more vulnerability into your life it would unleash a whole new level of personal strength and transformative potential.

Each dimension of Intelligent Leadership is both inside of and in front of you. It is something to be unearthed and something to be strived for. Both perspectives are true and both are important. So as you move forward in your efforts to become an Intelligent Leader, I encourage you to hold both. Understand that you can't become a better leader—or human being—without changing. At the same time, don't overlook the fact that your own potential greatness isn't somewhere outside of yourself. It's deep inside you.

BRINGING THE NEW INTO BEING

Regardless of where you land within the paradox of change, becoming an Intelligent Leader requires change. It requires bringing something new into being. Throughout the book, I've provided exercises and "igniter behaviors" that you can put into practice to help cultivate each dimension of Intelligent Leadership. I've kept these exercises general because, in my experience, there's no one-size-fits-all recipe for development. My goal has been to give you a deep sense of these fundamental qualities of great leadership and a set of tools that you can use to access and accentuate them in yourself.

As we conclude our journey here together, I want to leave you with one more exercise. It's a simple formula for bringing something new into being, whether it's a specific quality or an overall vision for yourself. You can use all of the steps in the process or just some. Whatever works for you.

The fundamental idea behind the process is that in order to become something new, it's helpful to have a vision of what that might look like. This vision is the North Star that helps you orient through the often difficult process of change. It crystalizes the goal you're shooting for, and gives you a sense of what, specifically, you need to do to get there.

I've used this process with thousands of people throughout my career, and also used it myself, and generated consistently good results. There are six simple steps:

1. *Visualize:* It's crucial that you have a vision of what you want to become. This can be something specific, like becoming a more dynamic communicator. Or it could be something more general, like becoming a better leader. Whatever your vision, it's important to spend some time to get as clear a picture as possible of what this "new you" might look like. The more details you can provide, the better. Not only will this visualization give you a goal to shoot for, but it will implicitly align you with the part of yourself that you are hoping to accentuate.

2. *Record and verbalize your vision:* Once you've clarified your vision, it's important to write it down, using all the detail you are able to muster. This will further concretize the vision and provide you with a record that you can return to as you go through the process. After you record your vision, you should read it out loud. There's something powerful about articulating something. Words have power, especially when spoken. When you hear your vision in your own voice, it does something to you. It makes things more real. It makes you accountable.

3. *Find the gaps:* As you review your vision, both written and spoken, pay attention to how it makes you feel. Are there elements that inspire you more than others? Are there components that make you feel uncomfortable or intimidate you? Your emotional responses can be a good gauge for where you are in relationship to your goal. These "gaps" between who you are and who you want to become are important. They are the areas of your vision need that may need the most attention moving forward.

4. *Make a list:* Once you've identified the "gaps" between you and your vision, make a list. Include some notes about why you added each item, including the emotional responses you may have had when you reviewed your vision.

5. *Commit to change:* While this may seem like an obvious step, it's one that many people overlook to their detriment. Just the fact that you've come this far in the process indicates that you are, to some degree, committed to change. But there's something powerful about

restating it. You can make a pact with yourself that you are committed to actualizing the vision that you've laid out for yourself and
addressing all of the gaps needed to get you there.

6. *Make an action plan:* Now that you've created and articulated your
   vision, found the obstacles to achieving it, and committed yourself to
   tackling them, it's time to make an action plan. I find that simplicity
   is key here. Action plans should have a simple introductory statement that states what you are committing to overall. They should also
   include at least one step that you'd like to take to address each gap
   you've identified. You can add timelines to any element of the plan if
   you want, but the main idea is to create an outline of action steps that
   you plan to use to get to your goal.

There you have it: a simple process for bringing a vision into
being. Of course, if you find that this process isn't right for you, no
problem! Everyone has a different approach to change. I encourage you to find and put into action whatever steps that are appropriate for you.

THE INTELLIGENT LEADER: A GUIDED VISUALIZATION

As we discussed above, the first and most important step in becoming something new is visualizing the goal. In that spirit, I'd like to
take a moment to go on a little journey with you. I want to guide you
on visualization of what it would look like to be a thriving expression of all seven dimensions of Intelligent Leadership—to be a truly
intelligent leader. Of course, these dimensions will express themselves differently in each individual. Like light shining through a
prism, these dimensions are meant to reflect the unique patterns
that characterize each of our hearts, minds, and souls. However,
there is still value in exploring what a universal Intelligent Leader
might look like to help inspire your own personal visualization. If
you'd rather do this on your own without my guidance, then by all
means, skip ahead to the next section. Otherwise, here we go.

Intelligent leaders are deeply connected to their core purpose.
They know, intimately, why they have been put here on this earth;

and this self-knowledge gives them courage to engage big ideas. Their groundedness in who they are at the deepest level makes it possible for them to express themselves in ways that are truly unique and that inspire others to think in new and different ways. They are pioneering thinkers, content with the understanding that they have but one life to make the biggest possible impact on the people around them.

Intelligent leaders understand strength to be something more than the volume of their voice or the breadth of their power. They know that true strength is exhibited when they are willing to take the risk of being vulnerable, with themselves and with others. Their openness surprises those around them, and it inspires others to follow their lead. They know that opening up is the gateway to transformation and the currency of strong and lasting relationships. They never lose sight of the fact that they can never achieve anything without the trust and partnership of others.

Intelligent leaders are those who hold the biggest possible context. They have cultivated an ability to transcend their own selfish tendencies by caring more about the many greater wholes of which they are a part. This gives them a rare kind of maturity and dignity. They feel an obligation to the mission, to their team members, and to doing their absolute best in every situation or circumstance. The breadth of their perspective creates space and confidence for others. People can take solace in the fact that they are involved, because they trust them always to make choices that benefit the most people.

Intelligent leaders understand themselves better than anyone else does. They know what unique natural talents make them powerful, and they know how to use them in the most appropriate ways. In that light, they see themselves—and everyone else—as perpetual works in progress. They understand that perfection is something to be strived for, but never fully achieved. This gives them the confidence and self-assuredness to face even their most pernicious flaws. They don't wince in the face of negative feedback, and they see their mistakes and shortcomings as opportunities for growth—to develop themselves so that they may be of better service to those around them.

Intelligent leaders know when it's time to act and when it's time to hold back. While others might be frozen by fear, apathy, or a lack of care, they are the ones who step up and do what's necessary to move any situation forward. Their courage is born of a deep pride in themselves, but not the stubborn kind of pride. They take pride in a job well done, and even more so when done in collaboration with others. Their action is always characterized by a deep passion for what they're doing and they inspire the same in those with whom they collaborate. They consider their work to be sacred, and therefore bring an uncompromising degree of precision to their activity. They are the person whom others always count on to do things when it matters most, and to do things right.

Intelligent leaders are awake. They are ever-aware of their surroundings and the context in which they are taking action. They remain focused on what is most important, even in situations where others let their guard down. They are impervious to distraction, because they understand the value of their time and attention. Their presence is magnetic. It helps to ground others, and holds them to a higher standard of care. They are the people others can rely on always to see things clearly, because their intentions are pure and they are therefore perceiving the most objective possible take on any given situation. They see what others can't or are unwilling to see.

Intelligent leaders know that the process of work and life is a never-ending puzzle. They are not fazed by missteps; in fact they seek them out, because they know that long-term success depends on their ability to course-correct. They hunger for learning. They strive for clarity. They are willing to change when change is necessary. They are comfortable outside their comfort zone. They are problem solvers, not necessarily due to any kind of intelligence or genius, but because they are the most willing to face problems, no matter how seemingly intractable.

I'm sure there were elements of this vision that spoke to you and some that didn't. There were likely qualities that are already

CONCLUSION: THE PARADOX OF CHANGE

strong for you, and others that could use some improvement. All of that is natural. We are complex. Intelligent Leadership looks different in each of us. I encourage you to do your own version of this visualization. If you were to master each of the seven dimensions, what would you look like? How would you act? Don't be afraid to be specific. Details are important.

If you can create a clear vision for yourself, you are well on your way to achieving it.

WHAT WILL BE YOUR LEGACY?

In one of the most important scenes in Arthur Miller's famous play *The Crucible*, the protagonist, John Proctor, who has been arrested for being a witch, is faced with an existential conundrum. His captors have given him the choice either to sign a confession that he is, indeed, a witch and be set free, or refuse to lie and be sentenced to death. In what is perhaps the most dramatic moment of the story, he chooses to die with integrity. When his captors ask why he's made this tragic choice, he responds, "Because it is my name! Because I cannot have another in my life!" His name—his legacy—is more important to him than even his own life.

Proctor's crucial decision gets to the heart of what Intelligent Leadership is all about. Of course, how you choose to pursue your own development as a leader, and a human being, isn't a life-and-death matter. But to me, the stakes are similar to those faced by Proctor as he contemplated how his actions would affect his integrity, his soul. I believe that the kind of leader you choose to be has huge implications. It's not just about you, or your personal wealth, reputation, or fame. It's about your legacy. It's about what kind of impact you will make on the world during your time on this planet. It's about your soul. When you are on your deathbed, what will you think about the life you have lived? Will you be at peace? Will you know that you did all you could to leave this world a better place?

This moral question is what Intelligent Leadership is all about. You can employ all the tactics, tools, and strategies in the universe, but if you aren't able to get in touch with this deeper sense of purpose, and then orient your life around it, then the impact you're able to make will be severely limited. The success you'll create will be superficial and mediocre, and true greatness will elude you.

This is the challenge of Intelligent Leadership. And it's also what makes it so special, and worthwhile. Intelligent Leaders hold themselves to a very high standard. They don't settle for power or charisma. Intelligent Leaders are overflowing with character, integrity, and altruism. They know that they are models for everyone who knows them, personally or otherwise.

At the opening of the book, we defined leaders as examples who others want follow. They are the lights that guide us. As we close the book, I want to encourage you to, once again, take that simple definition to heart. What kind of example do you want to be for your co-workers, your friends, your children? If humanity were to look to you for how a person should be, or live, would you be proud of what they saw?

Your answer to this question will, at the end of the day, determine your long-term success—in leadership, and in life.

About the Author

John Mattone is widely considered the world's top executive coach and is globally respected for his ability to ignite and strengthen a leader's inner self and talents. Since 2017, he has been ranked by Global Gurus as one of the top three coaching authorities in the world, alongside Tony Robbins and Marshall Goldsmith. John is the creator of the unique, powerful, and game-changing Intelligent Leadership (IL) Executive Coaching philosophy and process. Since 2012, John has used his proprietary coaching methodology with more than 50 global CEOs, top government leaders and professional athletes to help them become stronger, more effective, and vibrant leaders and people. John served as the executive coach to the late Steve Jobs, as well as to the former, legendary CEO of PepsiCo, Roger Enrico. In 2015, John's leadership system was named one of the top three Advanced Leadership Development Programs in the world, alongside John Maxwell's and Tony Robbins's work.

John is also an internationally acclaimed keynote speaker, presenting at events and to companies all over the world. Whether John is keynoting an event, conducting a retreat, or coaching an executive, he has earned a global reputation for possessing a special ability to unlock and unleash greatness in leaders at all levels.

In addition to being known for his leadership coaching, John is widely regarded as one of the world's leading authorities on corporate culture and culture transformation. A respected advisor to CEOs of small- and mid-sized entrepreneurial organizations and large global businesses alike, John provides guidance on how to create and sustain a leadership culture that drives superior operating results.

John is the creator of John Mattone University (JMU), which offers the unique and game-changing Intelligent Leadership Executive Coaching blueprint for success—accredited by the International Coach Federation. Since 2017, John Mattone has personally coached and certified over 400 global executive coaches from 52 countries in his proprietary IL philosophy, process, and tools. JMU also offers the 2.5 Day Intelligent Leadership Retreat, the CEO Aspire Elite Mastermind, The Intelligent Leader 4-Day Mastermind Immersion, as well a series of award-winning virtual and online leadership development programs. He is also the creator of a number of breakthrough leadership and culture assessments, including the Mattone Leadership Enneagram Inventory (MLEI), the 5 Cultures of Culture Assessment (5CCA), and the Cultural Transformation Readiness Assessment-40 (CTRA-40).

Since relaunching his business in 2010, after 15 years of corporate life, John Mattone has been on a mission to help current and future leaders, as well as organizations, to break through to become the best they can be. Perhaps the greatest testimony to John's core purpose and the realization of his dream are his many philanthropic endeavors, including his creating an annual scholarship fund in his name at the University of Central Florida, his alma mater, where in 1980 he graduated first in his class with an MS in Industrial/Organizational Psychology. The John Mattone Leadership & Coaching Scholarship will be awarded each year to a deserving Master's or Ph.D. student who shows great promise and potential in the field of coaching and leadership.

Since 2011, John has consistently been recognized by Globalgurus.org, Thinkers50, Forbes, CNN, Leaders Excellence, Warren Bennis's Leadership Excellence magazine, HR.com, and many others as one of the world's best executive coaches and speakers. He serves on the executive MBA faculty at Florida Atlantic University, where he also teaches his enormously popular Global

Leadership Assessment & Development (GLAD) course. Through this three-credit course, John has personally coached over 500 EMBA students. He also serves on the faculty at ZfU International Business School in Zurich, and is a Distinguished Senior Fellow at Hult International Business School, one of world's leading business schools.

The author of nine books, John has written three best-sellers: *Talent Leadership, Intelligent Leadership*, and *Cultural Transformations: Lessons of Leadership and Corporate Reinvention*. In 2017, John's blog was named the number one executive coaching blog in the world by Feedspot. His work has been featured in the *Wall Street Journal, CNN, Forbes, Fast Company, Businessweek, Inc* magazine, *MarketWatch*, the *Huffington Post, CEO* magazine, *ChiefExecutive.net, CLO* magazine, *CIO* magazine, the *Globe and Mail, Harvard Business Review*, and many other respected global news outlets.

Prior to his executive coaching work, John was the president of one of the top leadership consulting firms in the world, Executive Development Associates, Inc. (EDA). He holds a B.S. degree in Management and Organizational Behavior from Babson College and an M.S. in Industrial/Organizational Psychology from the University of Central Florida.

Index